READING CRITICALLY *at* University

Dedication

To Katie and Rachael on their graduation, and to Joan for a lifetime's support.

SAGE
Study Skills

READING CRITICALLY *at*
University

Mike Metcalfe

SAGE Publications
London • Thousand Oaks • New Delhi

SAGE Publications Ltd
1 Oliver's Yard
55 City Road
London EC1Y 1SP

SAGE Publications Inc.
2455 Teller Road
Thousand Oaks, California 91320

SAGE Publications India Pvt Ltd
B-42, Panchsheel Enclave
Post Box 4109
New Delhi 110 017

British Library Cataloguing in Publication data

A catalogue record for this book is available
from the British Library

ISBN-10 1-4129-0184-7   ISBN-13 978-1-4129-0184-0
ISBN-10 1-4129-0185-5   ISBN-13 978-1-4129-0185-7 (pbk)

Library of Congress Control Number: 2005932466

Typeset by C&M Digitals (P) Ltd., Chennai, India
Printed and bountd in Great Britain by The Cromwell Press Ltd, Trowbridge, Wiltshire
Printed on paper from sustainable resources

Contents

Acknowledgement

I would like to acknowledge the inspiration of Terry Robbins-Jones, who provided the environment to develop the pragmatic pluralism applied to this book.

Intent

Our quest is to find new ways of seeing the world.

Introduction

The need

What is the core competency of graduates? How do they distinguish themselves from non-graduates? What is their distinct competitive advantage compared with an experienced practitioner? Workplace experience can only be gained in the workplace, by those struggling amidst its day-to-day demands. This sort of knowledge is not born and nurtured in universities. So, what is?

This book is designed around the assumption that 'thinking' is the core competency of the graduate, more specifically, 'applied critique'. This means an ability to critique contemporary problems systematically and constructively, using multiple stances methodically. This is a core competency, which can later be thoughtfully evolved through experience in the workplace. Applied critique is knowledge that stands the test of time by providing the generic skill to evaluate any particular problem, technique, fad or common-sense solution that comes over the horizon, whether at home, at work or in your community. Graduation means developing this competency to critique tomorrow's problems constructively. This book aims to help with this task.

The alternatives to critique as a core competency of graduates have been overemphasised. Imparting enthusiasm intended to motivate lifelong absorption of new information is a popular teaching theory at present. This is commendable at one level but some skill in how to process this information is still required, especially given the ever-increasing volume of low-grade information being generated on the Internet, through the popular media and in some textbooks. A more sustainable competency is required to assist the graduate to deal with the ever-changing world.

This book, then, is for those who face the problem of wanting to develop their multiple-stance 'critiquing' skills. What is critiqued is not so important when developing the skill. It may be any written or spoken 'passage of words', an article, book, story, play, speech or a lecture. It could be a photograph, a film, a painting, scenery or a drawing. Often it is intended to influence you, like political speeches, employer's plans, community gossip and entertainment. Critique, however, is not just thinking to yourself, but also involves convincing and influencing others, hopefully as part of a process of improving the world. There is an intricate recursion between reading, writing and thinking, especially when interacting with other people. Therefore, this book takes critique beyond the stage of just thinking, to that of constructing critique statements which can be developed into a well-argued and coherent written critique. Thoughts can be improved by communication; the act of communication alters what is thought.

Human activity can be studied from a range of views, viewpoints, worldviews, perspectives, lenses, frames, conceptual frames, interpretations, methods, models, paradigms, theories, angles, approaches and stances. What is 'seen' involves some 'stance' taken by our brain to process the confusing multitude of messages that come to it through our senses: our eyes, ears, skin and noses. So a scientific stance would 'see' some human activity in terms of physical and measurable objects in motion due to some cause and effect. A feminist stance would see the same human activity through women's experiences, and a historic stance would see the events that led up to the activity. I have chosen the word 'stance' to represent this concept because it carries with it a hint of someone looking at the world, and a hint of ideology in the way they look. Also, many of the other words carry with them a bit too much baggage, including in some cases doubt that they can be easily altered. Can we jump meaningfully from one paradigm or one worldview to another? It will be assumed we can alter our stance at will. Each critique stance provides a different set of sensory inputs.

A further example may help. If people's motivation was being critiqued using the multiple-stance approach, then a 'social critical theory' (emancipation) stance would promote questions such as, 'Do they want to be motivated?' and 'Is employee motivation too divisive and not in their best interest?' A 'metaphoric' stance would encourage questions about the roots of the words. 'Employee' can be contrasted with 'colleague', 'mate' and 'expert'. The word 'motivation' would appear to have engineering roots, as in 'motion' and 'locomotion'. Perhaps a more social concept like encourage (from courage) would be more humane. A 'Marxian' stance might encourage questions like what the underlying tensions are that have created this condition of a lack of motivation. A 'systems' stance, on the other hand, would try and make explicit the purpose of the group, the purpose of studying the group and focus on the members' relationships with themselves and relevant technical artefacts.

Those students enthused by stances such as the empowerment of minorities, and the emancipation of the disadvantaged, are applauded, but may find this book insufficiently heroic. Feminism, history, culture, linguistics and critical social theory have developed their own unique critical stance on world events. These are not revisited here. Rather this book will be more suited to those with a desire to design complex socio-technical systems like their community, institutions or businesses; to improve the world through redesign. It is for those who appreciate the world as made up of designs which can and will be evaluated from numerous stances – some justifiable, some not. Therefore, its revolutionary zeal is in opposing a one-stance world. It wants instead to develop stance flexibility pragmatically. Put more directly, this book is intended for students of innovative and creative organisation, governance as designing human groups, rather than for students of literature, mathematics, injustice or revolution.

There has been some agonising over the title of the book. As will be elaborated later, the terms critique and critical are used informally as well as formally with potential readers, and the author is in no position to demand a standardised terminology. Here the 'literature' meaning of critical is the most relevant, as in the title 'film critic'. The word 'critical' is avoided in this book because it is rather discipline specific. In medicine it means 'nearly dead', in nuclear physics it means 'about to explode', in social theory it means to 'critique' society. In everyday speech is has negative connotations. Perhaps more relevant is why the author was tempted to present the book as creative problem solving, decision making, innovation, or creative design. This is because the practice of trying to critique some situation, by looking at it through artificially generated stances, is likely to result in novel insight. An example is provided by an old engineering problem of designing some way of allowing cross-country vehicles to traverse a deep ditch. By looking at it from a 'nature' stance the problem was solved as seeing it as analogous to rows of foraging ants needing to cross some gap. The ants lock together front and back in a line so as to lever the front ants across the gap, which then pull the rear ants over. A device was welded onto the front and back of the cross-country vehicles to enable them to do the same. This is creative design, creative problem solving using the same methods called here 'critique'.

This raises the ever-important question 'why'; why critique? Good educational institutions insist on it endlessly, even if they do not call it critique. Avoid an educational process that only provides you with information; rather your brain needs training in how to use information, how to think creatively from that information, how to critique. Critique provides more than creative solutions; it provides emancipation and a sense of freedom. Those who work in the stock market make good money from understanding the dialectic between information and insightful critique. For example, reading in the newspaper that the paper mill sales in some country are down may be critiqued as being a specific indicator of a forthcoming slowdown of the overall economy in that country. Not using paper means companies are not busy. Advantage comes from being able to read between the lines. These insights then need to be applied to some advantage. With financiers this usually means a simple investment decision. For us, this means using the insight to help people better design their world.

The book assumes that like sport and artistic skills, there are some basics that can be taught and practised which will improve everyone's capacity to think creatively, to critique. This skill involves first encouraging people to actively seek new stances on whatever is being thought about. Some people will have great natural talent for this and others will soar with the minimum of explanation. Some will not be impressed, instead seeking to explain everything in terms of one universal stance, while others will always have a rather deliberate style. This book with its 'how to' style and thirteen demarcated stances is in danger of itself being overly deliberate or instrumental. The author has tried to walk the narrow path between prescription and demonstration, but it is the reader's use of the book that will decide in the end. Please treat the book as merely a collection of examples, a few starting point suggestions, as possible pathways, not as a set of rules. The author therefore sees the whole book as an introduction, a sample, a taster to a skill that needs to be applied constantly throughout life and takes a lifetime to master. It is catch-up for those who have not yet developed an adequate, methodical, critical stance on what they see going on around them and what they say. Apart from appreciating the thirteen stances outlined in this book, a critical stance can be further practised through debate, reasoned argument and listening to the stances of minorities. In its grander intentions, this book tries to offer a life style; how you might want to study life. It is a hybrid between a 'how to', a reference and a life-style book.

The book was written because the author is trying to keep alive an extension of scientific thinking that science often says it rejects but in fact uses in its everyday work. This might be called pluralism, multiple perspectives, soft or critical systems thinking, irony or interpretivism. It is not relativism or non-justified post-modernism. But the author is reluctant to discuss these labels, preferring instead to offer practical advice on how to see the same passage of words from many different stances in a manner that a scientist would accept as rational. Doing this is a very important part of someone's education, not only to make them more creative and innovative but to make them more ethical, compassionate and understanding. To be able to see that other people sense things differently, that things can be sensed differently, is what being self-conscious is all about, what being human is all about. Rather than provide a lecture or speech on the need for multiple stances on the world's affairs, the book takes an inductive approach. It presents numerous situations described in short passages, and provides alternative stances in a deliberate, explained and controlled way. This demonstration is intended to lead by example, to show how the reader might put into practice the ideology that human activity should not be seen through one large theory of everything but rather through a nearly endless array of stances.

While the author has a particular interest in the creative powers of constructive dialectic argument, the other critique stances suggested in this book were selected from many hours of research critique seminars. These were small groups of mainly mature students who were required to critique research articles, four per week, as part of a first-year PhD literature appreciation programme. The early critiques were typically: 'I thought it was boring', 'I thought it was great' or 'I thought it was crap'. After discussion of the argument stance, they became better at seeking the argument in the article and whatever evidence was provided to support that argument. This, in a more elaborate way, is explained and presented as the first critique stance later in this book. As more literature was read by the seminar group, for example the soft systems literature, this was then developed into a stance to critique the later literature, and so on. It was thought there were two possible finishing lines. Miller's (1956) magic number seven suggests that seven or so stances would have been enough. However, this did not provide enough emphasis on how infinite the number of stances could be. Therefore, it was decided to call a stop at thirteen stances only because this is such a symbolic number. The downside of having so many critique stances is that the methodical reader will get overloaded, and the space to discuss each stance thins out.

Explicitly exploring a critique stance, rather than treating it as some kind of black box that generates questions, is considered to be very important. For example, if critiquing welfare or taxation using the stance of profiteering, power, poverty or liberty then these stances need to defined, bounded and contrasted. An analogy is if you are going to understand the inner working of a human body using ultrasound or X-rays then some understanding of the properties of ultrasound or X-rays is expected to improve understanding of the resulting images. While wanting to avoid an infinite regress, the critique stances need to be critiqued. As the main argument of this book is that thinking involves applying multiple, explicit, critical stances, too much regress has been avoided. Each chapter discusses a different stance, then suggests what questions such a stance generates, and finally provides possible responses to those questions, a critique.

What is critique?

Critique is defined in the *Oxford Advance Learner's Dictionary* (2003) as:

cri•tique

>   Noun: a piece of written criticism of a set of ideas, a work of art, etc.
>   Verb: to write or give your opinion of, or reaction to, a set of ideas, a work of art, etc.

My reservations about this definition are that it does not require a critique to be insightful and does not counter the common usage of 'criticism' as negative. While many writers have given up and now refer to constructive or negative criticism, a different form of defeatism is used in this book, that of referring to critique to mean insightful criticism derived from an explicit stance. Of course, knowing how it is defined does not explain how to undertake a critique.

To get a better idea of what critique is, and how to do it, read the boxed passage below and immediately record your response. What does the passage make you think about?

Whether you like it or not, try to record a series of statements on your thoughts about the passage; '*write or give your opinion of, or reaction to*' the passage.

> Why do dogs have a sense of humour but not cats? To understand you have to go back into the mists of time. Imagine a large pack of dogs huddled in a cave, the snow falling outside. They are tired, cold and hungry because the hunting over the last several days has been a compete failure. They need a sense of humour so one of the dogs can wake up cheerfully and say, 'Who's up for a bit of hunting today?' and survive the temper of the other dogs. On the other hand, cats wake up, feel hungry, go outside, kill something, eat it, and then go back to sleep. No fuss, no need for a sense of humour.
>
> Source: Gorman, 1988

It is useful for you to make explicit your reaction so as to contrast it with my own. Do not let the humorous stance of the passage distract from a serious critique. The passage raises some serious research issues. My list of statements relating to this 'cats and dogs' passage includes that:

- **It raises issues about the evolution of humour.**

- **It raises the complex cognitive issue of the role of emotions in decision making.**

- **It takes no account of the influence of the extensive artificial breeding involved with cats and dogs.**

- **It ignores that humour requires a high level of self-consciousness not present in either cats or dogs. Humans do not become self-conscious (able to see themselves as others do) until they are about 8 years old.**

These will be very different to your statements. That is not important except as a reminder of the beauty of using multiple stances when undertaking a critique. Rather, notice how each critique statement, yours or mine, comes from a different stance. For example, the first of mine sees an evolution issue in the passage, the second sees a decision-making issue with the rules of evidence, the third see issues around interfering in breeding and the last used the critical stance of self-consciousness. This generation of numerous critique statements from what might be called 'intuitive' or non-explicit stances (ideas that suggest themselves only when reading the passage) is commendable in its own right but it is not the approach taken in this book. This book uses multiple explicit stances, not intuitive ones. The two differences may need further distinction. Simply as a result of reading the passage, ideas come into your head. So, for some reason that is hard to explain exactly you may feel there is an unfair assumption in this passage that the dogs are living in an environment of snow and ice with few food sources, while the cats are living in a land of plenty. This then would be your intuitive critique of the passage, which may be labelled a 'fairness' stance. While you might not be able to explain in detail where this stance came from and intuitive leaps can be very creative, there is a danger that every critique you undertake will use the same stance. This is why this implicit stance approach is not what is being suggested here. Rather, this book explores the approach of setting up numerous explicit, upfront stances that have been thought through and then used to critique some passage.

For example, a 'critical–social' stance advises that the critique recognises any acts of oppression in the passage. Through this you may recognise that the passage can be seen to stigmatise cats as humourless. This, the critique may continue, runs the risk of justi-fying cruel exploitation and persecution of cats. The approach was to set up an explicit stance and derive a particular critique. Intuitive leaps are still necessary, but ironically, when using multiple explicit stances, they are often more creative. This is perhaps because using both forces the critiquer out of his or her comfort zone. An imposed explicit stance hopefully forces the critiquer to move away from his or her default or intuitive stance. This book will try and demonstrate that explicit stances can generate novel insights, by presenting numerous examples. The book is based on the belief that an essential purpose of critique is to think explicitly, consciously and inquisitively about the stance so as to generate novel and insightful critiques.

Learning from stances

The psychology literature which talks of frames, and the philosophy literature which talks of 'intentions', both suggest that experience and nature provide us with default or intuitive stances, or perhaps combinations of both. When people look at, hear, smell or feel the world around them then their past experiences, coupled with their instincts, act as a stance. Staying with the dog theme, if you had a lot of experience of uncontrolled dogs attacking passers-by, then you could be expected to interpret immediately the sight of a dog tied to a post differently to someone who has extensive experience of dogs being mistreated. This default or experience stance is clearly a useful thing at it enables us quickly to assess familiar problem situations. My doctor has an experience stance that the most likely cause of a cough is a chest infection. This saves him time in correctly diagnosing most coughs. However, when faced with a novel problem, or when a novel solution is required of a situation, then this experience stance can blind us. Insight and innovation seem to arrive when these default stances are challenged.

When I read the dogs and cats passage above I find myself intuitively wanting to critique it from the first stance of 'evolution' theory: does humour evolve, what is its role in species evolution, is it merely a by-product of individual survival reflexes? This tells me about myself, my real interest, my love of evolution theory and perhaps my concerns with the meaning of life. I appear to have a primary stance on the living world, sourced from my long interest in evolution theory. Can you label your intuitive take on the dogs and cats passage? To exercise our brain and to improve our critique skills we need to take time out to think about our dominant default stance. In my case it was 'evolution'. What are the rules of evolution? One rule includes that, 'more are born than reproduce'; this creates the selection process so necessary for evolution to occur. Can I use this rule to further my critique of the dogs and cats passage? The passage carries the assumption that dogs without a sense of humour will not reproduce and so humourless puppies will not get born. Being an effective critiquer of situations, be it tied-up dogs, coughs or much more complex social situations, is thought to mean at least trying to be aware of what, and perhaps why, you are adopting a stance. To undertake and get the most out of a critique you need to be aware of the stance you are using and to think about the limits of that stance.

Using an imposed explicit stance, especially one that you are a little uncomfortable with, is not expected to destroy your own intuitive creative skills. Just the opposite: the challenge may force you to take completely new intuitive leaps. For example, if I asked you to critique the dogs and cats passage from the stance of 'revealing inherent contradictions' then hopefully it would force you to do two things. One is to think about what is meant by 'inherent contradictions'. What are they, are there examples and types, what are not inherent contradictions? The other thing you might do in response to this imposed stance is force your brain to go where it has rarely gone before and try and synthesise this stance of inherent contractions with the hungry cats and dogs passage. Don't let the simplicity of the passage fool you. Having a challenging stance and a novel passage to critique can still act to exercise your thinking skills. This is a generic skill that is useful to deal with whatever problems come unexpectedly over your horizon at any time during the rest of your life.

Moving on, above you were asked to record 'statements' that came to you as a result of reading the dogs and cats passage. From an evolution stance at least two statements were generated. One was that the passage takes no account of the influence of artificial breeding, and the other that the passage carries the assumption that dogs without a sense of humour will not get to reproduce and so humourless puppies will not get born. It has been found useful to record thoughts resulting from a critique stance in this form. You may want to call them conjectures, propositions, tentative statements or critique statements. Perhaps the only advice on what form they take is to suggest they are 'truth statements', meaning they say something that is either true or not. Alternatively, make them into conditional statements. Even when critiquing from an explicit stance, statements may start as a rather random, non-mutually exclusive set with a mixed hierarchy. This is fine, but later they will need to be pulled together into a written coherent argument if others are to benefit from your insights. This often acts to cluster the statements usefully so as to suggest some more. This is discussed more towards the end of the book.

Having explained a little what is meant by critique and critiquing from a stance, it may be useful to end this introduction by discussing what critique is not.

- Many people don't, but a critique can be distinguished from a 'summary' or an 'analysis' and to a lesser extent from a review. To 'summarise' a passage is to prepare a shortened version, identifying what you interpret are the important points.

- An abstract is a summary, as is an executive overview.

- To analyse is to 'pick apart', to decompose a passage into what you interpret is a useful classification system. An analysis of a mark on the carpet could be its chemical composition. Analysis is seen as the opposite of critique. Systems thinking underlines this distinction by referring to the need both to analyse and to 'synthesise'. Critique as presented here involves a synthesis between the stance and the passage.

- To review something, to see it again, is very similar to how critique is being presented here if that second view comes from a new stance. I can review a department by viewing it from an economic stance rather than an efficiency stance. The only distinction from critiquing is that the intent with a critique is to provide some novel insight.

How to use the book

Given the number of critique stances suggested in the book, and that each is intended merely to be illustrative of other stances you may wish to develop for yourself, it is suggested that you:

1 Read a few chapters until you get a feel for the overall structure. Each chapter provides a different stance to think about a passage.

2 Put the book aside and carefully read the passage you intend to critique.

3 **Come back to book and scan the Contents page. From this select two likely looking stances, turn to the relevant chapters and read them. If you cannot decide which stances to take then throw a numbered hendecagon (eleven sides).**

4 **Use the questions at the end of the chapter to make statements about your passage. From these statements structure a response argument with supporting evidence. For more on how to write these see the later chapter on writing critiques.**

Many of the passages (presented in boxes) to be critiqued in this book are presented from what has been called a 'grey humour' stance. This has been done deliberately so as to keep the book easy to read and to appeal to a wider range of people. The idea was to stop it becoming discipline specific. By using 'grey cynicism' it is meant to make light of what might otherwise be seen as a sad situation. This should not distract from developing critiquing skills for what readers see as more serious or important situations.

1 Using Argument to Critique

Critique the following passage by highlighting the message, the point the passage makes. This might also be called the moral, the conclusion or the argument of the passage.

Few people will know where Invercargill is, the New Zealand one that is. It is a little town on the very southern tip of the real 'God's Own Country'. It must be a contender for the town closest to the Antarctic. For people growing up there in the 1950s and 1960s it must have felt fairly isolated despite the lovely countryside.

This story involves a young lad, about 11 years old, trying to make a little pocket money from a paper-round. You need to imagine a paper-round in Invercargill in those days. It involved going from one fairly remote house to another, often before dawn in the cold and rain. He did this lonely chore on his heavy old bicycle. One morning the lad arrived at the newsagent to pick up his papers and there was this dog he had never seen before sitting outside the newsagency. He noticed how very friendly it was, so he gave it a few strokes. On the way out the dog was still there, still being friendly, so the boy encouraged it to go with him on his lonely round. The dog looked extremely pleased and full of life. When the boy threw the first newspaper onto the porch of a house, the dog ran and fetched it back. It turned out to be a very long morning.

Is the claim, the argument, the passage makes:

- **that planning goes wrong, even in simple situations,**

- **that we need to reveal our own assumptions about situations,**

- **that if you persuade people or dogs into routines then a change in circumstances can turn a strength into a weakness, or**

- **that only people are self-conscious, animals and objects are not,**

- **that (and this one works for me) trying to influence others to your intent is problematic?**

There is no right answer; a critique is what you want to mention after reading the passage. The skill is being aware of where your thoughts are coming from. This chapter deals with the argument stance of critique which encourages your thoughts to come from first identifying what you thought was the argument made by the passage.

In the dog passage, the argument the passage is making is a bit vague. To note this can be part of your critique. In some passages the author can be very explicit about the argument he or she wants to make.

Those who believe that deterrence justifies the execution of certain offenders bear the burden of proving that the death penalty is a deterrent. The overwhelming conclusion from years of deterrence studies is that the death penalty is, at best, no more of a deterrent than a sentence of life in prison. The Ehrlich studies have been widely discredited. In fact, some criminologists, such as William Bowers of Northeastern University, maintain that the death penalty has the opposite effect: that is, society is brutalized by the use of the death penalty, and this increases the likelihood of more murder. Even most supporters of the death penalty now place little or no weight on deterrence as a serious justification for its continued use.

States in the United States that do not employ the death penalty generally have lower murder rates than states that do. The same is true when the U.S. is compared to countries similar to it. The U.S., with the death penalty, has a higher murder rate than the countries of Europe or Canada, which do not use the death penalty.

The death penalty is not a deterrent because most people who commit murders either do not expect to be caught or do not carefully weigh the differences between a possible execution and life in prison before they act. Frequently, murders are committed in moments of passion or anger, or by criminals who are substance abusers and acted impulsively. As someone who presided over many of Texas's executions, former Texas Attorney General Jim Mattox has remarked, 'It is my own experience that those executed in Texas were not deterred by the existence of the death penalty law. I think in most cases you'll find that the murder was committed under severe drug and alcohol abuse.'

There is no conclusive proof that the death penalty acts as a better deterrent than the threat of life imprisonment. A survey of the former and present presidents of the country's top academic criminological societies found that 84% of these experts rejected the notion that research had demonstrated any deterrent effect from the death penalty.

Once in prison, those serving life sentences often settle into a routine and are less of a threat to commit violence than other prisoners. Moreover, most states now have a sentence of life without parole. Prisoners who are given this sentence will never be released. Thus, the safety of society can be assured without using the death penalty.

Source: www.teacher.deathpenaltyinfo.msu.edu/c/about/
arguments/argument1b.htm

The author is presenting the argument that the death penalty prevents future murders. It is one side of the capital punishment debate. Identifying the argument by the author may be part of your critique; you could compare it with the argument you think the passage makes. For example, you might see the passage as an argument:

- **that the United States is behind much of the Western world in its attitude to capital punishment, or**

- **that it is sad that the author has to still make this argument in the twenty-first century.**

What argument do you identify in the passage below about the Napoleonic wars?

It's hard to imagine now but back at the time of the Napoleonic wars, as the British waited for the French invasion of Britain, the average villager in the North of England would never have seen a French soldier. They had heard that they were horrible, unnatural creatures, about to invade and slaughter everyone in their beds. Added to this, most of these same people would not have seen a monkey, as Africa was a long way off and there was a distinct absence of zoos, TV and printed picture books. Into this state of ignorance a ship sailed up the North Sea. During some bad weather, the captain's pet monkey, dressed up in a sailor suit, was washed overboard. It somehow made it to the shore whereupon the locals captured it. It was wearing a uniform and clearly not an Englishman, so the locals assumed it must be a Frenchman, most likely a spy for the invasion force. They tried to talk to the monkey but it only babbled back in what must have been French. They did the only right thing and hanged it in the town square as a warning to all other French spies. I gather the people who live in Hartlepool are a bit embarrassed by this bit of their history but I suspect that most English people have some sympathy for such a simple confusion of identity. In more recent times, the local rugby club has a hanging monkey as a logo on its club tie.

Like the dog passage, the argument does not appear to me to be explicit. This is not to say it does not have an argument. Every passage can be given an argument. Is it:

- **something about the public image of the French in 1800,**

- **that magistrates in Hartlepool are incompetent,**

- **about the importance of having appropriate court procedures for identifying prisoners?**

Moreover, is the argument hidden so as not to offend the residents of Hartlepool? The argument stance of critique encourages the reader to think about the passage in these terms. Other critique stances encourage different thoughts.

Explaining argument (the theory)

Philosophical history

The stance of critique that asks what argument you see in a passage and how well it does that has been with us at least since the Ancient Greek Socrates who lived some 2500 years ago. His ideas for how to distinguish good knowledge from bad is still the source of discussion on electronic bulletin boards today. By 'argument',[1] it is meant something akin to legal argument or reasoned debate, not quarrelling; its purpose is to validate knowledge claims. Socrates used a questioning form of argument where he asked people to state, in a short sentence, what they thought they knew. He would then question them in an attempt to test their claim. So, if we used the passage above about the paperboy's dog, rather than let the author present the whole passage, the Socratic method would first ask for the author's argument, what he or she claims to know. In this case it may be 'that companions involve you in extra work'. This would then be questioned to establish its validity. For example, 'What experience do you have with dogs?', 'What good experiences have you had with stray dogs?' and so on, depending on the answers provided. Therefore, the Socratic method provides one way to extend your critique of a passage. Having identified the argument (claim), you can ask yourself questions of the passage as per the paperboy's dog example. Does the passage explain the advantages of a dog in terms of companionship? Socrates' questioning method, perhaps due to Aristotle's concerns with questioning and with the invention of cheap printing, tends to have died out. These days we tend to adopt a style as per debating societies and law courts where the process starts by allowing each of the interlocutors time to present their 'case', verbally or in written form as a monologue. This needs to anticipate the counter arguments, the questions that are likely to follow from what is said. This presentation is then critiqued.

In modern times the philosopher Karl Popper in *Conjectures and Refutations* (1963) supports the Ancient Greeks arguing that the process of making and justifying an argument, to an appropriate audience, is the process that produces valid scientific knowledge. It tests the quality of what we know; perhaps it actually creates what we know. Numerous other philosophers have also supported this line, discussing how this language-based competition might be designed to ensure new knowledge is created and tested, while trying to ensure ineffective rhetoric and quarrels are avoided. These books include Perelman and Olbrechts-Tyteca's *The New Rhetoric* (1969), Walton's *The New Dialectic* (1998), Toulmin's *The Uses of Argument* (1964), Crosswhite's *The Rhetoric of Reason* (1996) and Eemeren et al.'s *Handbook of Argumentation Theory* (1987). Their concerns include how to exclude power from blocking open debate. Historically there is a lot of evidence of powerful social groups not wanting open and public debate, not wanting their claims countered or questioned. Given the millions of people who died as a result of this, such as from 'Nazi science' on race and 'Stalin science' on agriculture, this concern is very real. Therefore, this stance of critique carries with it implications for the identification of valid knowledge and for the emancipation and empowerment of 'others' – a heavy burden.

Identify the argument

A critique using the 'argument stance' starts, as was suggested with the passages above, from identifying an argument. Being such an important concept in Western thinking, the word 'argument' has numerous equivalents. Conceptually this is the same thing as the conclusion, the point, a proposition, a conjecture, a knowledge claim and perhaps the message, the moral and the purpose of a passage. If explicitly provided, the argument, as a one-liner, is normally identified as starting with the word '*that* …'. For example, *that* capital punishment does not stop murders. It may be stated at the beginning, at the end, both, not at all and indeed many passages (essays, presentations) are not really coherent enough for a critiquer to be able to identify any one argument. Hopefully there is the argument the author intended, but there may also be another one the critiquer wants to identify. The argument identified can only be the critiquer's interpretation of the passage.

There may be hidden arguments, ones you think the author would be aware of but was hiding and ones he or she may not have thought of. The task is not to read the author's mind, but rather to identify from the passage the argument you want to discuss. Different critiquers will identify different arguments, which make for the possibility of interesting discussion. In the paperboy's dog passage three possible arguments were identified. The death penalty passage was very focused, making it hard for me to identify more than the one clearly stated argument. The monkey passage is very much open for interpretation by the reader; perhaps the author's argument was that you should laugh.

Supporting evidence

An argument (conclusion) needs to be justified, supported with evidence. This evidence may be reasoning or observations (empirics).[2] The death penalty passage argued that the death penalty does not prevent future murders. This argument was justified using reasoning including that murderers are usually in no state of mind to care what the punishment is. The supporting empirical evidence provided was the murder statistics in various states, comparing those that do or do not use the death penalty. The passage also anticipates the counter argument's evidence of the findings of the Ehrlich report, where it says this has been discredited.

An argument is only as good as the evidence that supports it. The argument may not be novel but the supporting evidence can be. You may have often heard that the courts need to be very careful that they prosecute the right person; the monkey passage provides some refreshing historically verifiable evidence that mistakes have been made. The quality of evidence is not a simple or absolute thing. Science likes very exact measurement as its evidence; enquiry into complex social situations tends to put more emphasis on insight. Social enquiry is suspicious of how easily the eye is deceived and is very aware that seeing something occurring is very different to accurately appreciating the underlying social forces that are causing it to occur. Observations may be the basis of scientific evidence but for the social enquirers the intent is often to make different things happen as a result of their intervention. The only suggestion I have to help you decide whether or not the supporting evidence is adequate is simply to ask if it would be convincing to a knowledgeable audience. I would suggest that the evidence in the dog and monkey passages above was not as convincing as the evidence presented in the death penalty passage, which gains some authority from specifying sources. The issue of quality of evidence will be discussed in later chapters.

Anticipate counters

To distinguish reasoned, well-supported argument from an 'outlandish claim' the passage should anticipate and address the counter arguments. These counters need to be satisfactorily set aside, otherwise the argument will not be convincing to the critiquer. We are bombarded by one-sided argument in advertisements, political speeches, spin, and much of it is unconvincing. Therefore, after identifying the argument in a passage, the next task of the critique is to reflect on the counter argument. For example, in the death penalty passage above the argument was that the death penalty does not prevent future murders; the obvious counter argument is the negative form, that it is does discourage murderers.

The argument that the death penalty does prevent future murders

Society has always used punishment to discourage would-be criminals from unlawful action. Since society has the highest interest in preventing murder, it should use the strongest punishment available to deter murder, and that is the death penalty. If murderers are sentenced to death and executed, potential murderers will think twice before killing for fear of losing their own life.

(Continued)

(Continued)

For years, criminologists analyzed murder rates to see if they fluctuated with the likelihood of convicted murderers being executed, but the results were inconclusive. Then in 1973 Isaac Ehrlich employed a new kind of analysis which produced results showing that for every inmate who was executed, 7 lives were spared because others were deterred from committing murder. Similar results have been produced by disciples of Ehrlich in follow-up studies.

Moreover, even if some studies regarding deterrence are inconclusive, that is only because the death penalty is rarely used and takes years before an execution is actually carried out. Punishments which are swift and sure are the best deterrent. The fact that some states or countries which do not use the death penalty have lower murder rates than jurisdictions which do is not evidence of the failure of deterrence. States with high murder rates would have even higher rates if they did not use the death penalty.

Ernest van den Haag, a Professor of Jurisprudence at Fordham University who has studied the question of deterrence closely, wrote:

Even though statistical demonstrations are not conclusive, and perhaps cannot be, capital punishment is likely to deter more than other punishments because people fear death more than anything else. They fear most death deliberately inflicted by law and scheduled by the courts. Whatever people fear most is likely to deter most. Hence, the threat of the death penalty may deter some murderers who otherwise might not have been deterred. And surely the death penalty is the only penalty that could deter prisoners already serving a life sentence and tempted to kill a guard, or offenders about to be arrested and facing a life sentence. Perhaps they will not be deterred. But they would certainly not be deterred by anything else. We owe all the protection we can give to law enforcers exposed to special risks.

Finally, the death penalty certainly 'deters' the murderer who is executed. Strictly speaking, this is a form of incapacitation, similar to the way a robber put in prison is prevented from robbing on the streets. Vicious murderers must be killed to prevent them from murdering again, either in prison, or in society if they should get out. Both as a deterrent and as a form of permanent incapacitation, the death penalty helps to prevent future crime.

Source: www.teachers.deathpenaltyinfo.
msu.edu/c/about/arguments/
argument1b.htm

This passage presented the case for the death penalty preventing future murders; it says that this is its argument and at least makes an attempt at presenting some credible supporting evidence.

To repeat, an argument can be critiqued for not presenting both sides, i.e. all the known evidence. It should present both sides and then conclude on balance in favour of one over another. However, notice how the two passages on the death penalty only present the 'for and against' supporting evidence. The argument is made by considering whether murderers *should, or should not*, be executed. This is a good start but for a more insightful critique it may be noted that all the alternatives have not been fully explored. For example, could a counter be made that it is important the state takes responsibility for satisfactorily resolving close family's desire for revenge, in order to stop old blood feuds between families which have in the past crippled nations for generations? Arguments merely for or against something are in danger of being 'sideswiped' by alternative thinking. This problem will also be discussed again in later chapters.

Surprising

An argument can also be critiqued for its 'surprise' value, its novelty. Arguing that the sky is blue would not be very surprising, novel or insightful. Arguing that it was red in the early stages of the earth's development might be. You may have heard the arguments for and against the death penalty before and feel the above passages added little to your knowledge. What about the monkey passage? Could you critique that for not being very novel, insightful or even, or as the philosopher Karl Popper requests, risky? One of the classic examples of a surprising argument was mounted by Galileo. This partly explains why his name is still so well known. He argued that the earth was travelling (racing) through space at thousands of miles an hour. This was when nobody had a concept of space as being very different to the earth's atmosphere. It had to be moving at a significant speed if the earth was travelling around the sun once every year. You can imagine Galileo was at risk of being ridiculed as people called upon common sense to prove that the earth is not moving; there is no sensation of movement, no wind in the hair. Part of Galileo's solution was to show that if a weight is dropped by a rider on a stationary horse it falls to ground directly below where dropped, i.e. between the front and back legs. If the rider then gets the horse into a gallop forward and then holds out an arm and drops the weight, it lands in the same place relative to the horse's front and back legs. This suggests when you are also moving as fast as the earth then there will be no sensation of movement relative to the earth. Galileo presented a surprising argument which he had to support with reasoning and observation (empirical) evidence.

Falsifiable

An argument can also be critiqued for not being empirically falsifiable. I could argue that God is a woman but there is no primary empirical (through your senses) evidence I could bring by way of supporting this argument. This falsification issue was important to Popper who suggested that if an argument (knowledge claim) cannot be empirically falsified, then it is perhaps an argument outside the definition of rationality, a spiritual matter. He used this idea to challenge Freud's arguments (explanations, theories) about dreams and anxiety causing certain physical conditions. It is not possible even to seek for disproving evidence. The impossibility of countering an argument using empirical evidence is another approach that can be used to critique other arguments.

Definitions

A passage should also not fail to convince you that its argument is justified merely because of the poor definition of some key words. Technology, sociology and medicine are disciplines that have developed their own extensive vocabulary. History has not. It is the obligation of the author to communicate clearly with the intended audience, so a passage can be critiqued if it uses ill-defined terms. The greatest danger occurs when a word has several meanings and the reader is not alerted to which one the author is using. For example, the word 'critical' means negative, exact, nuclear, urgent and emancipatory. Passages using this word need to make it clear which meaning they are using. Scientists have spent many centuries defining their 'technical' terms but in social enquiry an author may need to spend some effort defining, bounding and contrasting terms and concepts.

Audience

A critique using the argument stance needs to pay careful attention to who is talking to whom and why. A reasoned argument needs at least two people. A written piece is seen as the author(s) presenting his or her argument to some specific group of people. This may be an unknown audience but rarely is it a universal audience (everyone). For example, the very fact that it is written in English will severely restrict the number of people who can receive the passage. The death penalty passages were written for teachers to provide to their students by the 'Michigan State University Death Penalty Information Center'. The dog and monkey passages were written for a very Western audience. Thinking about who is writing to whom is a useful way to raise critique questions about the passage. Does it provide enough background, will the intended audience be convinced, and who is being excluded? The arguers need to introduce themselves and their expertise in this area.

Importance

A further issue that needs to be considered in an argument stance critique is that of its importance. Is the argument important, to whom and who says it is? Put another way, what is the author's motivation for writing the paper, the motivation for why you might want to bother reading the paper? What was the problem the paper was addressing and is that problem significant to the audience? Appreciating the author's assumptions about these issues may assist in your appraisal of the argument and the supporting evidence. It should also assist you in anticipating where the evidence may be weak. In the paperboy's dog and the monkey passages the motivation may well be humour, with no intent to insult, perhaps with some intent to educate. Given how important you think humour is to quality of life, this may or may not be an important piece to you. The death penalty passage is very different. It takes itself very seriously; death is implicitly presented as a very serious and important issue. None of the above passages takes time to explain explicitly why the argument is important.

Critique questions

Summarising from the discussion above, a critique using the simple argument stance would ask questions somewhat like the ones presented below.

Argument

- **What do you see as the argument (conclusion) of the author?**

- **What was the author's insight, i.e. was the argument novel, risky, open to falsification?**

- **What argument do you see in the passage?**

Definitions

- **Are all key words well defined (described)?**

Audience

- **Who are the authors?**

- **Have they established their expertise?**

- Who is the intended audience?

- Is the paper explicitly persuasive to this audience?

Evidence

- What evidence can be brought to support the authors or your argument (conclusion)?

- Is this evidence convincing, novel, insightful?

- Has the counter argument been fully considered?

- Were there any observations that support the argument? Could there be?

The problem

- What was the problem the argument addressed?

- Is it an important problem; for whom?

- Does the passage solve a problem?

An example

There is one point of view that 'hatch, match and dispatch' religious rituals (birth, marriage and death ceremonies) are about managing anxiety. Marriage, traditionally between teenagers, meant children; the ritual was intended to be performed before conception, as it's too late afterwards. Bearing children is a huge, almost irreversible, responsibility subjecting the parents to many years of commitment, often hardship, albeit worthwhile to those with access to adequate finances. The Church of England ceremony is a 'solemnisation' of marriage; the marriage is the sex. The traditional words of this ceremony emphasise that an important decision is about to be made and should not be made when drunk or wanton. The ritual is designed to make the couple stop, before sex, and think that something major may happen. How many 15-year-old mothers would have benefited from this

(Continued)

(Continued)

advice? Public vows are made to close friends and relatives, not for the promises but more to slow down the wantonness. The potential child will need twenty years of stable parenting, so the ceremony also serves to get the couple to think twice about whether they want to remain committed to a family for that long. Given the present distinction between acts of sex and childbirth made possible because of contraception, and the increased age of couples, it is understandable that the ceremony seems less relevant. Funeral rituals, like marriage rituals, are the same in the sense they can be seen as a community's attempt to manage the anxiety of individuals, in this case by trying to reduce the anxiety rather than heighten it. Comments like 'they have not really gone, if we remember them' support this view.

Argument

The argument of this 'rituals' passage is clearly stated in the first lines:

> There is one point of view that 'hatch, match and dispatch' religious rituals (birth, marriage and death ceremonies) are about managing anxiety.

It may be novel to those who give more spiritual significance to religious services, less so to social anthropologists who will see the passage as rather a too simplistic summary of rituals which also have social and hierarchical dimensions. It may be possible to see an implicit anti-spiritual argument in the passage. Is it arguing that religious rituals are merely social ones not in need of a spiritual dimension? That aside, the argument is empirically falsifiable in that you could do something like a thorough review of the words spoken at such rituals looking for evidence of agreed anxiety management phrases.

Definitions

For those of a Western background there seems little in the language that may be confusing. Words like ritual, vows, anxiety and management might be challenged. Does the word 'ritual' automatically carry connotations of thoughtless process; are vows promises or public statements of present intent; what is the difference between anxiety and sadness or joy? Does the word 'management' reflect the modern managerialism of an increasing globalised world? Do social leaders 'manage' their community or simply take advantage of its demands?

Audience

Details of the author are missing. He or she would appear to have lived in England, partly because the term 'Church of England' was used rather than Christian or Protestant Church. Further, the colloquialism 'hatch, match and dispatch' does not sound like a literal translation and indicates some comfortable flippancy with human life cycles and spiritual ceremony. The audience would appear to be English Christians with some interest or experience in wedding ceremonies. It would appear to be a passage aimed at those considering marriage. Tagged on the end seems some concern for those who are not given sufficient closure at a funeral. The passage may be of interest to those considering designing their own life ceremonies.

Evidence

The evidence provided to support the argument uses two types of evidence. The first is in the form of the audience having past experience of going to or thinking about the purpose of weddings or funerals. This is coupled with their understanding the threat of deciding to commit to a relationship in marriage. Alternatively those who have been calmed by a funeral ceremony may understand how it could alleviate anxiety. The second type of evidence used is the highlighting of the words in the Church of England marriage ceremony documentation. This evidence is the sort you can 'take to court'.

The problem

The problem addressed by the passage is that of the purpose of some life cycle rituals. For those concerned about marriage or a funeral this may seem relevant. The piece makes no attempt to explain how important this topic is to whom. However, in the topic there is a vague implicit concern that these ceremonies take into consideration people's feelings.

Summary

This chapter has argued that passages can be critiqued using the ancient knowledge validation stance of argument. This involves first identifying an argument, either what appears to be the author's intended argument or an implicit one identified by the critiquer. Is this falsifiable and/or novel? Having identified an argument, the critique could continue by identifying the quality of the evidence presented to support that argument. Further, the importance of the argument may be commented upon, as might the apparent audience and the background of the author.

Exercises

1 Critique the following passage using the argument stance.

'Why aren't people more grateful when you point out how wrong they've been?'
(Pot Shots: http://www.ashleighbrilliant.com/index.html)

2 Critique the following passage using the argument stance.

In the nineteenth century a Hungarian, Ignaz, working in Vienna discovered that if
he washed his hands in a chlorine solution between assisting a woman with child-
births then the mums didn't die. He thought he had made a wonderful discovery
and that everyone would be desperate to hear his news. But when he tried to
explain it to his colleagues they thought he was a complete and utter idiot. They
could not understand what he was on about despite the fact that he could
demonstrate that the mortality rate fell from something like 30% to almost zero.
They were totally unimpressed; mind, he was a foreigner working in the medical
sciences. How did he end up? Did science prevail and the truth get out, making
him famous within his profession? Not in his lifetime; rather it shortened his life.
As he continued to insist that doctors wash before touching patients he ended up
losing his job, and then his mind. He died young knowing everyone around him
thought he was arrogant and insane.

(For a fuller account of this story see:
http://www.whonamedit.com/doctor. cfm/354.html)

2 Using System Thinking to Critique

I can think of the phenomenon of a chicken, as a chicken or as a system. As a chicken it is like a picture, an object, a large bird, feathers, two legs and a face. As a system it is a process, things go into it and come out of it, food, water and DNA are transformed into a scratching machine, eggs, feathers, a sandwich and a parent. (See Figure 2.1, source unknown).

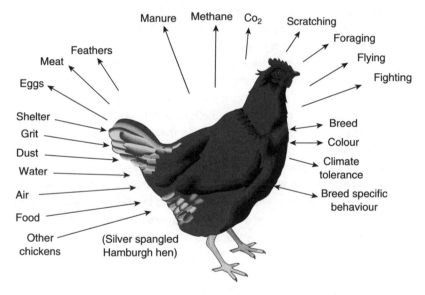

Figure 2.1 Chicken as a system

Transforming

At its simplest level system thinking involves thinking about something as part of a system that has inputs and outputs, which transforms things from one form to another (food to eggs), using various components (stomach, uterus, skin, etc.) which interact with each other to assist the transformation. The workings of the human body could replace the hen as an example of a thing being thought of in systems terms; the respiratory sub-system works with the dietary systems, the nervous sub-system and the blood circulatory sub-systems to assist the whole system, a critiquer, to transform a written passage into an insightful critique.

Critique the following passage by identifying the system depicted in the passage:

- **Identify the object under consideration as a system (a process).**

- **What are the inputs, the outputs, the components?**

- **What is transformed from what to what?**

> In our global mechanised world it is almost impossible to appreciate the human lives that go into everyday things. Imagine the thousands of people's working lives that have gone into getting a tin of baked beans onto the supermarket shelf. I've been a bean counter (accountant) in a bean factory. It was huge, old, cruddy, and located in the miserable urban decay of the back streets of London, surrounded by disused canals and railways. Twice around its perimeter was literally a marathon. When the raw beans came into the factory they had to be sorted into big ones, little ones, and black ones and white ones. Have you ever noticed that the beans in your tin are identical in size? They do not grow them like that. The bean trucks arrive with beans from all over the world – Canada, India, South America – arriving at street level to unload onto conveyor belts which move the tons and tons of raw beans indoors to rows of automated sorting machines. Under these sorters are chutes for the rejected beans which drop down into the basement where some lonely old man passes his day slowly attaching and removing large sacks to and from the ends of these chutes. When the sacks were full he would load them onto trailers ready to be sent to the piggeries. You can imagine the life of this lonely little bloke who worked in that miserable basement room, no windows, cigarette hanging out of his mouth, withered, bent over, newspaper open at the sporting page, cheap radio in the background, thirty-five years' service, punctual in taking his tea breaks, so typical of the slave classes grateful to secure a regular job in the globalised economy. He was most likely comfortable enough with the job, the boss rarely visited and he was not out in the winter weather. So long as the job got done no one would ever notice he existed. One day someone was walking past the entrance to this part of the basement and noticed piles of beans bulging up the stairwell. This looked unfamiliar so an investigation was started. It took some time and considerable bean shifting to establish what had happened. The poor man had died. The beans had kept coming, filling the room, burying him and eventually overflowing up the stairwell.

One system that I identify is that of the bean factory, in particular the bean sorting part of the factory. The inputs were raw beans, labour and capital equipment in the form of trucks, conveyor belts, sorting machines and chutes. The outputs of the bean sorting system are acceptable beans, and, down the chute, rejected beans en route to the piggery. The old man was a component in this system, one that moved the reject beans from the chute to the piggery trailers; he is the only human component identified. Mixed raw beans are transformed by the machinery and the person into sorted beans.

Thinking of the passage in system terms has introduced a new image that can be used in a critique of the passage. In a system view, the man is a component, not a feeling human being to be protected from social forces greater than himself. He is dehumanised, compassion is excluded through association. A system view has the man as a victim oppressed by mass consumerism and the machinery of large-scale manufacturing. The man is presented as a product of his environment. In the criminal law courts we do not do that. We prosecute individuals as individuals, not as components in a social system. While your childhood, your social environment and your role in a criminal syndicate may be mitigating circumstances, you as an individual are considered responsible for your actions. This would be a non-system view.

The main advantage of system thinking is to shift thinking from the object to an inter-relationship of components; from the old man to the manufacturing system he is merely one part of. That insight, that he can be seen as a standalone individual or as a component in a system, provides the first level of critique using system thinking. This is a similar switch from cognitive psychology to social psychology. From the early 1960s to the mid 1990s psychology placed emphasis on the individual, on the importance of an individual's personality, cognitive styles and intelligence to deal with situations. Researchers like Milgram (1992) and those interested in small-group performance started to show that human behaviour is very situational. Much of what we do is because of the situation we are in and who we are with. For example, attitudes to risk are very different when at home compared with when attending a race meeting. Seeing someone as part of a system goes a long way to seeing them differently.

A further example of view shifting by using system thinking comes from problem solving. If a group of people are blaming each other for some problem, then it is sometimes possible to see things differently if someone suggests the problem is not any one person's fault but rather a fault of the system. Plagiarism has been debated in this way. Is it the individual 'loser's' fault or rather an obvious outcome of an education system that has made class sizes too large, required students to compete for very high scores, made lecturers too busy to set more novel and non-repetitive assignments in the context of rapid text communication through email, the Internet and word processors. My point is not that either view of plagiarism is right but that by switching from an individual view to a system one a more insightful critique is possible. The baked beans man might have been seen as getting all he deserved for not eating better, getting more exercise, making more effort to improve his education and for not making an effort to develop relationships at work or home.

The dimension of transforming can also be used to consider the passage as a whole. How does the passage transform the readers? Perhaps they have a better idea of the effort in human lives that goes into their everyday foods. What are the inputs and outputs of the passage; are these validated? The inputs include the author's experiences and care for the lives of workers; are these inputs reliable? The story may be told for humour, not for compassion. The outputs include the conclusion to the passage. What is it? Perhaps, that most people live very ordinary lives.

Connections

System thinking has a few different dimensions which are related in the sense they aim to change the way you think about things. A new viewpoint provides a new way of critiquing. The next dimension outlined here is centred on the idea of 'connections'. The components in a system are connected. The bean sort is connected to the chutes, my heart is connected to my liver, the accounts department of a university system is connected to the teaching schools, and the tax collection department in the Westminster system of government is connected to Parliament. Ackoff (2000), a long-standing writer on the use of system thinking to come up with innovative solutions to problems, emphasises the importance of using 'connectivity' to shift people's appreciation of a situation. He often draws on the example of car parts. If you own a Toyota Corolla and need a new carburettor then you would not buy a Rolls-Royce carburettor as a replacement. It would be inappropriate given the other components in your Corolla as a system. A component needs to be thought of in terms of how it connects with other components. For people a little less mechanical, these connections are called social networks. Rather than seeing a person as an entity it is possible to focus on their social network. Who do they know, how often do they see them and what do they talk about? At work, or socially, they may be the focal point of a tightly connected group of twelve people, or rather they may be loosely connected to two rather distinct social groups so occasionally act as a 'liaison person' between these groups.

This focus on connections can be used to see a passage differently, to critique it. Critique the two passages below in terms of connections:

> There is a story told around the British Rolls-Royce engineering works that Boeing, the American aircraft company, once very carefully sent Rolls-Royce what you and I would describe as an aluminium drinking straw. It was about a foot (30 cm) long, with a hole down the middle about 2 millimetres in diameter, like a drinking straw.
>
> *(Continued)*

(Continued)

Boeing had machined this thin rod out of a block of aluminium and then drilled it down the centre. Boeing sent it to Rolls-Royce as proof of its precision engineering skill. I gather aluminium is not an easy metal to use for this sort of high-precision machining and drilling work, partly because it is hard to get a very pure sample. Drilling out the 'straw' required some very specialised vacuum chamber lathe equipment.

Rolls-Royce's version of this story was that after examining this work and admiring it, the engineers re-drilled it down the centre so as to enlarge the centre-hole diameter. They then made and slotted a smaller brass 'straw' as a lining inside the aluminium one, such that the original internal diameter of the aluminium straw was not changed. It looked like a silver straw lined with a brass straw. Then they sent it back.

A few years back, men wearing earrings upset an inordinate number of people. An institutionalisation of this concern included the procedure for a blood bank collection agency. In the days before quick, cheap blood testing for HIV (AIDS) the agency responsible for screening blood donations was concerned with how to minimise the risk of collecting infected blood. The agency issued instructions to the nurses doing the screening to discreetly vet the male donors for any physical indication of homosexuality. One suggestion was that they should check to see if they were wearing an earring in their left ear. This was to be discreetly noted on their record card so their blood donation could be quickly disposed of when they left the clinic. The marked card then became a permanent record of someone being a possible homosexual at a time when there was considerable social and legal discrimination against homosexuals.

Apparently, the practice of working men wearing earrings is quite old. It has been suggested that sailors either started or popularised the practice. The understanding was that if a sailor was washed overboard and drowned, whoever found the body was rewarded for giving the body a decent burial with the gold in the earring.

Critiquing these passages using the 'connections' stance could stimulate numerous different critiques. The one that comes to my mind is that they present two worlds linked by a common object. In the first passage the two worlds are the British Rolls-Royce engineering company and the American Boeing engineering works, two worlds linked with a common respect for precision engineering, symbolised ironically by a metallic drinking straw. It does not matter how true it is; the message is one of respect for the pursuit of engineering expertise. In the second passage the male earring provides the link from a sad present involved in avoiding death from AIDS to a sad past where sailors sought a respectful burial. Using this connections stance on the baked beans story may suggest a man isolated from fellow humans by a mechanised manufacturing system, his only connections being with machines that are indifferent to his personal needs.

This system dimension of connections can again be used to think about the article as a whole. What is the article connected or not connected to? Perhaps you think both articles are men's histories, not connected to women. Perhaps, for the more quality minded, they make you think about quality, of engineering skills and of transfusion blood. Do they remind you of something else you have read or seen?

Purposeful activity – intentional minds

Critique the following passage, in terms of participants' purposeful activity.

At the end of the Second World War there was the massive problem of moving the British economy from a war footing to a peacetime one. Numerous manufacturing plants had been changed from making domestic products to instruments of war. Planes, tanks and gun manufacturing were employing millions of people. In order to assist with the changeover, temporarily, manufacturers were instructed to keep making their war output until a smooth transition could be thought through. A period measured in months was imagined. Adding to the complication were two wartime requirements for armament manufacture. The first was a decentralised manufacturing process to avoid risk of an entire production process being ruined by one bombing raid. The parts for the guns, tanks, etc., were made in small plants all over the country. Second was the need for secrecy, which meant that no one plant had an overall appreciation of the supply chain of these weapons. Orders came from coded 'customers' and deliveries were made to small warehouses from where they were picked up when the supplier was not present. So, it is easy to see how the oversight was made. During the transition period those responsible for the collection of the battle-ready product were instructed rather than to dispatch them to a military unit, to deliver them back to the iron smelting foundry which was at the beginning of the supply chain. This caused little concern to the iron smelting foundry. It had always included 'rejected' weapons and melted them in with raw iron ore. It made rods and bars to supply to the sub-assembly manufacturers. So, as a temporary measure, the supply chain was a closed loop. Manufactured goods were delivered to customers who were paid to deliver them to the iron foundry.

The Second World War ended in 1945. In 1984 it was discovered that one of these closed loop supply chains was still operating. Somehow in the millions of arrangements for closing down the loops, and given the secrecy of the supply chain, this one was missed. For nearly twenty years the government had been paying for a particular type of field gun to be made, stored for a while and then melted down to be made into another gun, and so on.

What made this passage a little 'humorous'? Given the suggestion to look out for purposeful activity perhaps you identified that the temporary manufacturing system had lost its *purpose*, or rather that the *intent* of the post-war administrator had gone astray. The original intent, the driving force, behind the administrators setting up the closed loop supply chain was to keep people in employment for a few months while the peacetime economy was established. Consideration of 'purpose' is another dimension of system thinking. Separately, evolutionary philosopher Daniel Dennett has written about *The Intentional Stance* (1989), pointing out that this is perhaps a unique character-istic of the large human brain. The concepts of purpose and of intention are similar. They have to do with having an appreciation of why, the explanation, the reasoning, the driving forces, for wanting to do something. They differ from goals, targets, objectives, visions and missions which are perhaps more about 'what' rather than 'why'.

A passage can be critiqued in terms of its purpose (or the author's intentions). What were the 'driving forces' behind writing the supply chain passage? The great thing about this simple question is that a moment's thought makes you reply, 'it depends'. In the context of this chapter it is to provide an example from which 'purpose' can be dis-cussed. If told in a pub, then the purpose would have been to amuse. If told as part of a government policy meeting its purpose might be to argue for more decentralised policy oversight. Moreover, within the passage, the issue of 'purpose' changes. The pur-pose, driving force, of the closed loop supply chain was to smooth the transition to a peacetime economy. This sounds like good policy. However, over time this purpose diminished in its reasonableness. Therefore, critiquing a passage using the 'purpose' stance encourages thinking about 'driving forces' but also about the numerous different points of view involved.

Appreciating purpose or intent is an emergent property of intelligence; it is part of being self-conscious. Boulding (1956), one of the seminal qualitative economists, argued that simple systems cannot be said to be engaged in purposeful activity. Does an alarm clock have any 'driving forces'? He suggests not. A human can give the clock's designer a purpose, to make a device to wake people up on time, and per-haps the owner's purpose is not to be late for work. In the weakest form a radar-guided missile system may be said, by some, to have 'driving forces' in terms of its electronic feedback circuits re-targeting the missile as the target tries to evade it. Moving up the scale of complexity, does a jelly fish or a dog have driving forces? It would seem to be easy to say they have genetic ones to eat, reproduce, and so on. Given our language skills, other 'higher order' driving forces may have emerged from the large human brain, such as the ability to predict the purpose or driving forces of others. It allows us to predict which way a hunted animal might go by our appreciat-ing its driving forces; the animal must be feeling hot, hungry, thirsty, want to protect its young, may be trying to mislead us. This can become, 'If I do this then they will do that.' So, perhaps, critiquing by thinking about the driving forces of others is a unique human act.

Use the 'purpose' stance to critique the following passage, focusing on the purposes of the participants in the story rather than the author.

My high school was a naval training school in North Wales. Above the entrance of the school was a quote from its most famous ex-pupil and poet, John Mansfield. It was, 'We went down to the sea in ships, the lonely sea and the sky.' He knew what he was talking about. One of the interesting things about this old-fashioned British private school was the mental state of the officer–teachers. Many of them were ex-merchant-navy seamen. I was at the school in the early 1960s so many of these officers had spent the Second World War in the convoy system going back and forth across the freezing U-boat-infested North Atlantic. Apart from some of the images recounted in books and films like *The Cruel Sea*, most people have little appreciation of how dreadful the war in the Atlantic was for these seamen. It was boring, stormy, cold, dangerous – just plain miserable. Many merchant seamen spent the war ploughing back and forth from Europe to North America carrying war materials. One of our officers was teaching us about lifeboats, their design specifications, the regulations on provisions, and so on. There was a bit of a rumour among the cadets that this particular officer had nearly perished in a lifeboat full of nurses which was lost in the North Atlantic after their ship had been torpedoed. Now to 14-year-old cadets this sounded like utopia; in those days nurses meant young women. But once when we managed to get the officer to talk about the experience it soon became clear from his white face, and slight shake, that it was a dreadful and harrowing experience. He had to deal with the cold, the thirst, the hunger, the fear, in an overloaded, unstable, waterlogged boat, responsible for issuing rations and deciding who he would allow into the boat and who not from those hanging on the sides. Rescue could not be assumed, and many of the nurses had been badly burnt or choked by the fuel oil that spread on the sea surface after a ship was torpedoed. He could have only been in his twenties at the time. When he was eventually rescued everyone just laughed at his good fortune of being lost at sea with a boatful of young women.

The participants in this passage who would be self-conscious enough to be considered as purposeful and as being able to appreciate the purpose, drivers or intent of others I identify as: the cadet, the officer–teacher and the nurses. While there are numerous purposeful actions going on, including survival, one that I feel may provide a novel critique of this passage is that of *learning*. This may be used to critique the passage by identifying conflicts in the intent to learn or by identifying a common purposeful activity. My critique of this passage is, therefore, that all the participants can be seen to have a common desire, that of wanting to learn. The cadet's purposeful action for talking to the officer–teacher can be interpreted as wanting to learn about the risks of a future life at sea. The officer's driving force can be seen as *learning* how to live with the experience he had in the lifeboat: teaching the next generation of sea-goers not to romanticise the experience of a sinking ship. The driving force for the nurses in the lifeboat can be seen as *learning* the rules of survival from the young officer in charge of the lifeboat; how are they to deal with the others in the lifeboat, the life and death decisions, the hunger, the cold and the feeling of helplessness? The passage can be seen as a learning story.

Analyse and synthesise

Another dimension of system thinking which again involves shifting your point of view involves zooming in (analysis) and zooming out (synthesis) of the situation depicted in a passage. In the lifeboat passage, *analysis* of the situation would involve thinking about the details in the situation, such as weather conditions for the lifeboat, the rations, the numbers of people and their injuries. *Synthesising* the situation involves zooming out of the scene to get a new, wider view. This may result in your thinking about the overall strategy of the war in the Atlantic, perhaps its effectiveness, looking for statistics on how many ships were sunk over what dates. What were the survival rates of crews of torpedoed ships? This information could be a comparison with casualities and conditions for soldiers fighting on land at that time. The critique would reflect on the passage from this wider view.

Critique the following passage using the stance of first analysing the situation, then synthesising it.

> Crossing the Pacific in an old merchant ship used to include film-shows on deck, at night, to take advantage of the tropical sea breezes. Not a mosquito in sight, but the problem with the tropics is that you get a lot of rain showers. From the bridge of a ship these appear as columns of water falling from individual small dense clouds. When a film was being shown it was the duty of the person on the bridge to steer the ship so as to avoid these showers, and so avoid the crew getting soaked. The ship moved at about 17 knots, and the shower clouds often moved at much the same speed, criss-crossing the course of the ship. It required a good sense of timing to adjust the ship's course by a few degrees in anticipation of the path of a shower cloud to neatly weave around all the columns of water. On a warm tropical night, with one of those huge full moons, all alone in the middle of the Pacific, it was a slow-motion ballet, an excellent memory.

The analysis may include commenting on the physical possibility of a 17 knot ship outrunning a shower squall. Alternatively it might ask about the safety to other shipping or the damage being done to dead-reckoning navigational calculations given the repeated change of course. An overhead awning may have been more sensible. A synthesis might have drawn analogies with airliners changing their altitude to avoid turbulence when passengers are being served a meal. It may be the same as people in a car choosing a longer but scenic route over a boring but quicker highway.

Again this dimension of system thinking can be used to compare the entire passage with something else you have read or seen. Perhaps some phrase in the passage reminds you of something (analyse), or you see the passage as the same as a group of other passages (synthesise).

Boundary

Critique the following passage by noting what is included and what is excluded. What is the boundary?

> We rented a farmhouse from a wonderful man, Ron, who farmed sheep in New Zealand. When my young daughters saw newborn lambs wandering about his farm bleating for their mothers they asked him if they could feed them, make them pets. Quite rightly he pointed out that if they did that when the lamb and mother were in a good relationship they could be responsible for the mother rejecting her own lamb. However, there was often a lamb or two whose mother died and he would find one for them to care for. Many of these orphan lambs died despite all good intentions, either because they also turned out to be very weak after the birth or because they had failed to get that crucial first feed from their mother. I gather this sets up the stomach of the lamb. However, a little later in life these pet lambs face yet another risk because a few months of being hand-fed by humans scrambles their survival instincts. Untamed sheep know to run away from people. Pet lambs know the opposite. They run towards people who call out to them, thinking there is a free feed about. So, some less-than-desirable people know that if they are driving past a mob of sheep and fancy a feed it was well worth just standing at the edge of a paddock and calling out. The non-pet lambs run away but the pet lambs run towards whoever is shouting. When close enough they got banged on the head and quickly thrown into the car boot.

One of the other dimensions of system thinking, and perhaps what really separates it from the assumptions of the physical sciences, is 'boundary'. A system is bounded; it includes some things and excludes others. The education system includes schools, universities and lecturers but excludes emergency services. Anything known about a system only applies to that system. The education system may be having a funding crisis while the emergency services systems could be over-funded. What is known is not universal; rather it is bounded by the definition of the system under consideration.

The boundary is chosen by the person thinking about a system. When thinking about an organisation as a system the most common way of bounding it is by legal employment and ownership relationships. These are recorded in its financial records. However, when thinking about product supply chains, a different boundary may be used. Sales staff's relationships with suppliers, and the buyer's relationship with suppliers, may be included and administrative staff excluded. By shifting the boundary a new view of the system comes to mind. Another example would be first thinking about your family as a system with parents, children and relatives as the components. Then change the boundary and think just about children as a system in their own right. The components may now include school, television and friends. This process of changing how you view a system is similar to the idea of zooming in and zooming out (analysis and synthesis) discussed above. However, it encourages more options in terms of views by redefining systems in terms of focusing on the components of one system, making these into a new system view. In the family system, children are at first only one component of the system. Then the boundary is changed and children are then thought of as an entire system in their own right.

Returning to the pet lamb passage, the life of pet lambs in this part of New Zealand might be chosen as the system boundary. In this view the lambs are seen as central, vulnerable and under attack from inadequate mothering and hungry passers-by. By imagining new systems from these components other systems emerge, e.g. the 'other' lambs, farmers and the passers-by as systems. From each of these systems as a viewpoint a different critique of the passage is possible. For the farmers the pet lambs are not financially viable owing to the cost of the hand feeding and the risk of theft. From the view of the other lambs, the pet lambs are 'spoilt', unable to sustain themselves in the world. From the view of the passers-by, they could argue they are only weeding out of the gene pool those with mothering problems, as nature was trying to do in the first place. They are discouraging the farmer from being tempted to breed from the lambs when older.

The boundary dimension of system thinking may also be used to critique the entire passage as a story. What can be bounded in with the passage? What group of stories does it remind you of? What stories are totally different?

Critique questions

The above discussion might be summarised into a series of questions you might ask yourself about a passage.

Transforming (inputs and outputs)

- What are the inputs and outputs of the passage?

- What processes are involved in the passage?

- What gets transformed from what to what in the passage?

- Why is it transformed?

- How is the reader transformed?

- Are the outputs of the passage, the conclusion and recommendations fully justified?

Connectivity

- What is linked to what in the passage?

- Is there an identifiable social network in the passage?

- What is the passage connected to?

- What is its place in the literature, discipline or topic?

- What else has the author done?

- What does the passage remind you of, how does it sit with what else you know?

- What other evidence is available?

- What ripple effects will it have on wider systems?

- What do you see as the wider system on which it will have the largest impact?

- What genre, enquiry tradition and school of thought is it from?

Purpose

- What are the driving forces behind the actions of those in the passage?

- What is the driving force of the author?

- How else might the author's purpose (intention) have been achieved?

Analyse and synthesise

- **Do the details (facts) in the passage seem plausible?**

- **What details are missing or too inexact to be meaningful?**

- **What is similar to the passage?**

- **What does the passage remind you of?**

Boundary

- **Is the passage complete, does it present a self-contained story?**

- **How can the passage's contents be seen differently by rebounding the story around components of the passage?**

- **Are all the issues and concepts raised well defined and scoped?**

Summary

This chapter has suggested that a passage, written or spoken, can be critiqued using the dimensions associated with system thinking. These were transformation, connections, purposeful action, analysis and synthesis, and boundary. There are other dimensions to system thinking so these are only indicative of how a problem-solving stance might be turned into a critique stance. Examples of how the dimensions discussed might be applied were provided, although, again, this can only be thought of as indicative. For more on system thinking see Midgley's four-part collection (2003).

Exercises

1 **Critique the passage below using system thinking dimensions.**

One night we heard a crash outside. We guessed yet another car had driven off the winding road that passed by our house. Normally they went over the small 6 foot (2 metre) precipice into the tide trying to avoid driving into the cliff face on the other side of the road. We rushed out to help and found a car sitting in a few feet of seawater with the driver calmly at the wheel staring forward.

continued

continued

The local farmer, the nicest man you could meet, came up and told us not to worry, he knew the man in the car. He was drunk. The farmer waded out and knocked on the window offering to help. The driver slowly looked around and then suddenly started to shout, 'I don't want any bloody help from you, I'd rather bloody drown.' The farmer then waded back and with a smile said that there had been a misunderstanding between the two of them some years before.

Apparently, the farmer had been out helping with the birthing of new lambs when an unknown Red Setter had come bounding up to him very excited by the new lambs. A dog's presence worried the ewes, which meant they might abandon their lambs. Things got worse when the dog picked up a lamb and ran off. A short while later the dog returned and took another lamb. Naturally, the farmer went off to the village pub to ask if anyone knew the dog. The local lads, mostly farmers themselves, were angered by the report of a rogue dog. There were strict laws about dogs not being allowed near sheep at lambing time. Although the farmer tried to settle them down they rushed out, got their guns and waited in the paddock until the dog reappeared. They duly shot it.

That night the farmer got a knock on his door and the distressed owner of the dog was standing there holding two healthy lambs he had found in his front garden. He knew nothing of the shooting so was concerned that his dog was not at home. Clearly the man was extremely fond of his dog, very anxious for any news. The farmer explained that the dog had been shot. The man went ballistic, calling the farmer all sorts of names. It was the dog owner who was in the car, sitting waist deep in the tide.

2   **Critique the passage below using system thinking dimensions.**

A Consultant's Report

This report has been prepared in response to the question: 'Why did the chicken cross the road?'

Deregulation of the chicken's side of the road was threatening its dominant market position. The chicken was faced with significant challenges to create and develop the competencies required for the newly competitive market. MBA Consulting, in a partnering relationship with the client, helped the chicken by rethinking its physical distribution strategy and implementation processes. Using the Poultry Integration Model (PIM), MBA Consulting helped the chicken use its skills, methodologies, knowledge, capital and experiences to align the chicken's people, processes and technology in support of its overall strategy within a Program Management framework. MBA Consulting convened a diverse cross-spectrum of road analysts and best chickens along with MBA consultants with deep skills in the transportation industry to engage in a two-day itinerary of meetings in order to leverage their personal knowledge capital, both tacit and explicit, and to enable them to synergise with each other in order to achieve the implicit goals of delivering and successfully architecturing and implementing an enterprise-wide value framework across the continuum of poultry cross-median processes. The meeting was held in a hotel by the sea setting, enabling and creating an impactful environment which was strategically based, industry focused, and built upon a consistent, clear and unified market message and aligned with the chicken's mission, vision and core values. This was conducive towards the creation of a total business integration solution. MBA Consulting helped the chicken focus its change in direction.

Source: unknown

3   **Critique the passage below using system thinking dimensions. Hopefully you will provide a different critique from when this passage was used in the argument chapter.**

Few people will know where Invercargill is, the New Zealand one that is. It is a little town on the very southern tip of the real 'God's Own Country'. It must be a contender for the town closest to the Antarctic. For people growing up there in the 1950s and 1960s it must have felt fairly isolated despite the lovely countryside.

This story involves a young lad, about 11 years old, trying to make a little pocket money from a paper-round. You need to imagine a paper-round in Invercargill in those days. It involved going from one fairly remote house to another, often before dawn in the cold and rain. He did this lonely chore on his heavy old bicycle. One morning the lad arrived at the newsagent to pick up his papers and there was this dog he had never seen before sitting outside the newsagency. He noticed how very friendly it was, so he gave it a few strokes. On the way out the dog was still there, still being friendly, so the boy encouraged it to go with him on his lonely round. The dog looked extremely pleased and full of life. When the boy threw the first newspaper onto the porch of a house, the dog ran and fetched it back. It turned out to be a very long morning.

3 Using Pictures to Critique

At the beginning of this book the comment was made that a critique could be of a picture but this book would concentrate on written passages. This chapter turns this around somewhat by asking for a picture in place of the critique statements. Try and draw a picture of the following passage. It may be like a photograph representing the scene painted by the passage. It may be more abstract, perhaps reflecting your emotional response to the passage. It may be more functional, perhaps representing the activity portrayed in the passage.

> Back to the baked beans factory again. When the beans have been washed and cooked they had to be rechecked for the black and cracked ones just prior to tinning. This was too hard for the sorting machines, so there was a row of what is sometimes called 'direct labour' in overalls and hairnets, leaning over a continuous conveyor belt of hot steamy beans spooning out the 'cruddy' ones. The people that worked this part of the factory knew how dreadful their life was. When a passer-by winced one attempted to recover some self-respect by kidding with them: 'Hey it's worse than it looks' or 'The company is funding a psychologist to train pigeons to do this job'. The pigeon idea was completely a joke, as there was a feasibility study going on that imagined pigeons in nappies and chained next to the production line, conditioned to only feed themselves on the cruddy beans. How distressing. To lose your job to a computer is bad enough, but these people were worried they would be replaced by a pigeon. In the 1960s numerous industrial psychologists were experimenting in training all sorts of animals, such as rats, horses and pigeons, using Skinner's response conditioning methods to take over production work. Perhaps the computerisation of labour is a blessing in disguise.

I do not have a lot of artistic experience or talent but I searched the Internet for a picture (Figure 3.1) that was close to the impression generated in me by the passage.

This picture is of Australian women during the Second World War sorting stringless beans (not baked beans) in a manner which seems similar to the passage. I was looking

Figure 3.1 Leeton, NSW. 8 June 1943. Women seated on cases beside a conveyor belt at a food canning factory sort through stringless beans and remove any defective ones. The revolving cylinder in the background automatically nips the end off the beans (Australian War Museum Photo 14932). Reproduced with permission.

for something that portrayed monotonous labour, which I would find unpleasant. The picture alone does not do this as in wartime these 'battlers' may have willingly undertaken the work as part of a national enthusiasm to assist the war effort. If the women had experienced the hardships of poverty then also perhaps the work would be welcomed. Moreover, the quality of the experience may have depended on such things as the state of the women's physical health, their attitude to repetitive work and the friendliness of co-workers. I know of some who would be annoyed at my assumption that the work is somehow 'sad', pointing out that those involved are engaged in honest labour.

Alternatively, the passage may have been represented by the picture of the woman in Figure 3.2 which might be called 'a happy battler'.

However, note how these 'photographs' that I have chosen to reflect my emotional response to the passage are very much my interpretation, my critique. The choice of picture denotes a stance or critique. If the picture had been very modern, with clean and cheerful working conditions, a different critique would have been made. Figure 3.3 for example provides a different image of factory work.

Figure 3.2   Woman with vegetables

Figure 3.3   A pretty factory

Why pictures?

Most readers will have heard of the old proverb that a picture is worth a thousand words. Look at a map, perhaps a street map of a large city, and think how long it would take to write out in words what is being shown in that picture. If I showed you one of Monet's paintings of the flowers in his garden and then asked you to write what you see, I am sure you would agree you could not possibly do it justice. On the other hand, words can create pictures in our mind's eye, as in a poem or the lyrics of a song. There would appear to be parts of our brains that deal with images, a part which primarily processes sight, connecting it to our decision-making and emotional mental functions. Other parts deal with other functions like language. Creative thinking would seem to include shifting thoughts around these different functions of the brain. For example, if I asked you to draw a picture of 'democracy' then this requires you to move a word from the language part of your brain to the image processes part, initially causing some dissonance. The same is true of asking you to draw a picture of the beans passage. A dissonance occurs which is perhaps the opposite of being asked to find words to express a Monet painting. Dissonance makes the brain struggle for understanding, or at least suspends judgement. All of this suggests that this might provide a fruitful area for seeking insightful critiques.

Representative pictures

The picture of a passage of words does not need to be 'photograph-like'.

The pictures presented so far have been 'photograph'-like except the last one which was more of a cartoon. All the pictures may need to be supported with some explanation. Notice how a cartoon can take out a certain amount of reality. It becomes hard to attach strong emotions. So the cartoon of factory work can be contrasted with the Second World War picture. The cartoon can be thought of as idealising the harsh working conditions of the factory in a way that may not encourage improvements.

Extending the cartoon or representative style of critique picture, the Skinner box in Figure 3.4 could be presented ironically. It was mentioned in the passage but suggesting the rat's

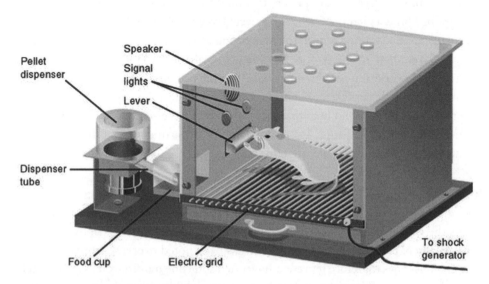

Figure 3.4   A Skinner box. Reproduced with permission of McGraw-Hill (www.mhhe.com/socscience/intro/cafe\psucafm.htm).

world is analogous to the bean processing women's world could provide a strong statement about the need for improvement.

The beans passage also made me think of flow, the long flow of beans and the short repetitive cycles of the process workers. Using this idea suggests the alternative representative picture of a flowchart. This is used to show things like the flow of materials through a factory, paperwork processes, data flowing through a computerised information system and organisational routines. Flowcharts show the movement of things from one place to another. Figure 3.5 shows the example of a fairly elaborate flowchart of Florida's criminal justice system.

Working in such a system would be complicated, requiring some thought about how best to go about various problems that arise on a daily basis. It seems somehow appropriate to contrast the working environment of the bean's processing women with the justice system. The very simple flowchart of the bean passage might look something like Figure 3.6. I have tried to add a little something with the extra thick black line to indicate the repetition in the job, having always to return to the conveyor belt.

Notice how clinical or dehumanising this flowchart presents the life of the women. Also note how a comparison of the justice system flowchart and the bean process might be used to make a statement about the repetition and simplicity of the bean processors. There may be a further contrast to make between this simple flowchart and the faces of the 'battlers'. The faces show the more human side of harsh working conditions.

Another representative form of picture that might be used is a socio-metric network or sociogram. This is a picture of 'who is connected to whom'. It has been used to track how a rumour travelled around a small town, to trying to appreciate the social network of the 'pilots' who crashed into the World Trade Center. It aligns with the viewing society more in terms of the connections between people than the people themselves. The example in Figure 3.7 of the three clusters might depict three sections of a department. The nodes denote people and the solid lines that they talk to each other regularly. The broken lines might indicate that the people see each other at a department monthly meeting. The picture stance hides physical location for (in this case) regular communications.

It is sometimes useful to present the nodes of a sociogram as nodes around a circle. Shown in Figure 3.8 is an example, where the nodes are rooms in a house. The lines across the circle represent some sort of relationship between rooms. In this example it is the traffic of people between rooms that has been noted over a short period of time. The diagonal lines therefore represent how often someone moved from, say, the kitchen to the dining room. The types and thickness of the lines represent the quantity of traffic between these rooms.

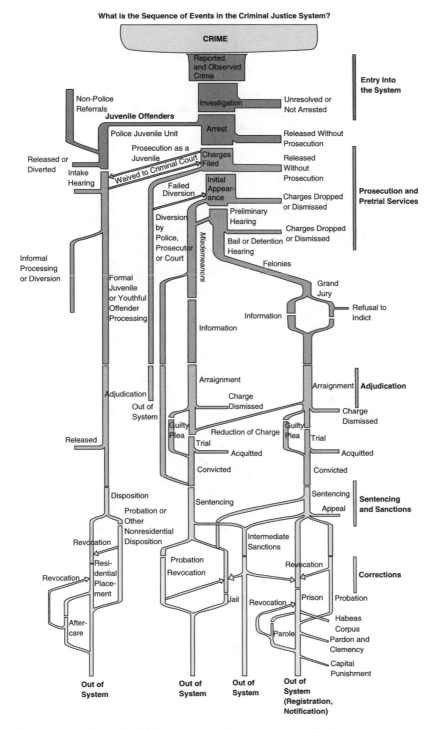

Figure 3.5   Justice flow chart. Reproduced with permission of US Department of Justice, Bureau of Justice Statistics (www.ojp.usdoj.gov/bjs/welcome.html; accessed 12 September 2005).

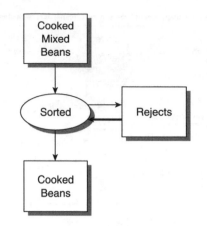

Figure 3.6   Bean flow

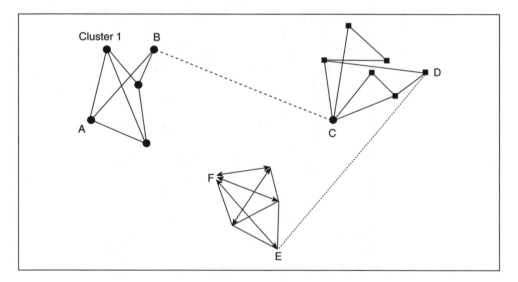

Figure 3.7   Small worlds

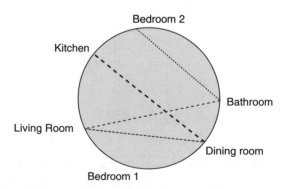

Figure 3.8   House network circle

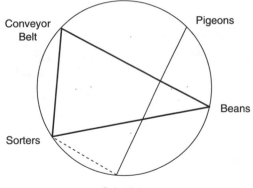

Figure 3.9   Bean network circle

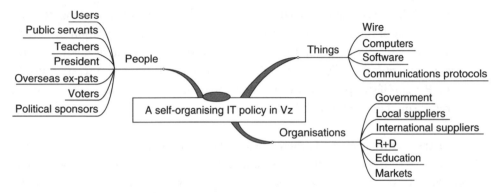

Figure 3.10   IT policy mindmap

Shown in Figure 3.9 is a second circle which is my attempt to represent the beans passage. The choice of nodes and connections is my choice, my interpretation of the passage and thus my critique of the passage. Hopefully the picture, either as it is being drawn, or when complete, will generate thoughts, even insights, about the passage.

For example, the circle was intended to represent the strong relationship between the conveyor belt, the beans and the sorters, perhaps with the scientists not fully aware of the world of the bean sorters.

With mindmaps the topic or problem is written in the centre box and the various issues becomes 'tentacles' off this centre. Sub-topics are listed off the tips of the issues tentacles. In the example in Figure 3.10 I was interested in thinking about how one might design an IT policy for Venezuela using self-organisation theory. It uses a stance that will be discussed later where the problem is divided into the people, things and organisations affected by the IT policy. Details of these are listed on the ends of the three tentacles.

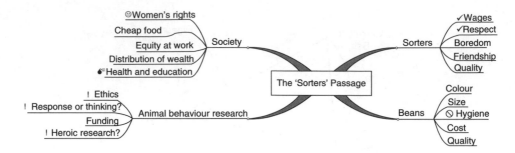

Figure 3.11   Beans mindmap

Figure 3.11 is my attempt at a mindmap of the cruddy beans passage. Of course it could have been drawn in many different ways.

This form of picture is meant to encourage structured but expansive thinking, to make the drawer think of more and more related issues, and show their relation in a structured manner. This particular mindmap has almost become a content analysis of the passage, rearranging the verbs, nouns and concepts contained in the picture onto the tentacles. Perhaps if two people drew up mindmaps from the same passage or story, and compared them, they would reveal different intuitive stances.

Many of the picturing methods mentioned so far have used a 'box and line' design. Checkland (2000) is well known for encouraging a different form of picturing that has become known as 'rich picturing'. Checkland's original and very restricted intentions for rich picturing have been breached in the wider business community by Bronte-Stewart (1999). Its purpose has become to align stakeholders into a common perspective about some situation. It seeks to identify the connections between the things in a situation, but tries to give symbolic meaning to these 'things' by showing them 'metaphorically': vulnerable person, important person, established institution, excessive bureaucracy and so on; 'icons' which have some significance to the drawers. The example in Figure 3.12 is called a rich picture by Bronte-Stewart and is typical of most pictures now drawn under that name. It is intended to show some person's or group's impression of a mining company's operations and relationship with the government and the community (with thanks to John Venables). However, these types of pictures are to help group dialogue, not to produce a finished picture that someone not at the discussion would understand. Therefore it is not really relevant if you understand the mining picture. It is a bit like walking into a room recently used to conduct a meeting where there are scribbles left on a whiteboard. They mean little to the newcomer but may have been very useful to those who drew the scribbles while discussing some complex issue. Figure 3.13 shows another example provided by Daellenbach and Flood (2002) of the dilemma about how to get to work (his desk). Thought bubbles can be useful to show concerns. Note that he presents the picture in terms of a contradiction, a paradox, a tension which he calls a dilemma.

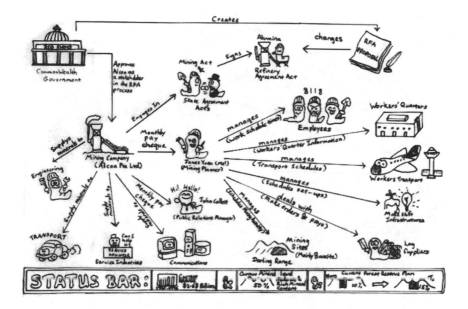

Figure 3.12   Mining industry rich picuture. Reproduced with permission from John Venable.

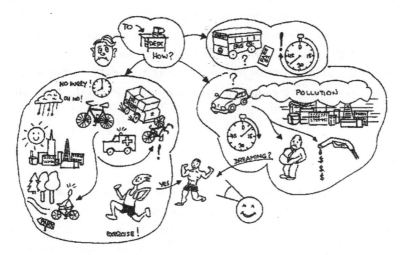

Figure 3.13   Rich picture of dilemma for going to work by bicycle. Reproduced with permission of Hans Daellenbach, REA Publications.

Looking for such a tension in a passage may help you in drafting a critique picture. This presents a picture of a very well-known dilemma so you can perhaps 'read it', but again that is not how the picture should be judged. Rather it did help align the thoughts of those present when the picture was drafted.

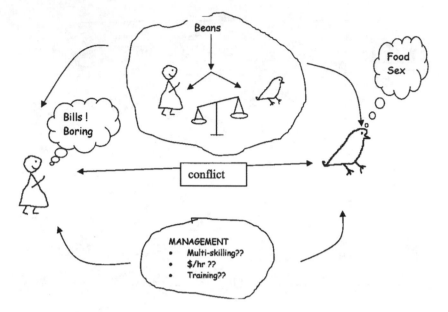

Figure 3.14   Beans rich picture

Most rich pictures are not as well drawn as Figures 3.12 and 3.13. For example, more typical is the simplistic attempt at drafting in Figure 3.14 a 'rich' picture of the 'cruddy' beans passage. The centre box was drafted during a discussion about the tension between the women and the pigeons. The 'woman' thinking about paying bills was drawn during a discussion about the other tension of having to work for money to pay the bills. Management's intentions were captured in the bottom circle and the arrow added when connections were discussed.

Summary

This chapter has briefly introduced the idea of using pictures or contrasting pictures to provide a critique. It is expected that a picture will need supporting explanation if it is to communicate the critiquer's interpretation. Photographs and various line and box diagrams were provided as examples. Given the availability of images on electronic search engines and bibliographic databases it should be fairly easy to find appropriate pictures. However, the use of methods like rich picturing has the advantage of forcing the artist to think methodically through a passage during the process of drafting. Perhaps after drafting the picture and explaining it to others the critiquer might use the experience to think about drafting some critique statements. For more on picturing problems see Alexander (1964), Gao (2005) and web sites like: http://systems.open.ac.uk/materials/t552/ index.htm and http://www.cul.co.uk/software/istruct.htm.

Exercises

1 Critique the following passage using pictures.

Tattoos can be seen as a form of macho jewellery. Modern film stars have made them fashionable, I assume because they add yet more visual interest to their largely visual representation of the world. But half the world seems to love tattoos and the other half hates them. Apparently King Edward VII had numerous tattoos and King George a blue and red snake on his arm. Traditionally though, in the Western world, rightly or wrongly, tattoos are associated with low income levels and a lack of social status. Tattoos are relatively cheap, and if you live in a violent community they cannot be easily stolen. They project a strong image, a strength of character, if for nothing else than showing the wearer was able to bear the pain of the needles. That tattoos give status to the wearer gives rise to an interesting little theory about body glorification. The New Zealand Maoris are well known for their very extensive tattoos on both men and women. As I understand it they enable Maoris to carry their ancestors with them. The Maori tribes did not have the same concept of ownership as Westerners. Typically, it was not possible for a Maori to build up individual wealth. The tribe shared everything so possessions could not be used to give someone status. Status could only be achieved through a reputation or by impressing others with the spectacle of your body. Tattoos were one such spectacle. This may explain why some people with low self-esteem wear outlandish hairstyles and go in for body piercing. It is an achievement in the absence of anything else that will earn them some respect.

2 Critique the following passage using pictures.

There is a tale used by law lecturers to distinguish between suing someone and disliking them. It also demonstrates how moral and functional messages get mixed. The tale goes that a man needed to mend the roof of his house. He was worried he would fall off so he tied a rope around his waist, looped it around the chimney and tied the other end around the tow bar of his car. While he was working his wife came out of the house and drove off in the car, dragging him behind. One can imagine what was going through the mind and mouth of the man when he first realised what his wife was about to do. After the death of the man, his wife arranged for a solicitor for their children who, deprived of a sponsor, needed a new source of income. They sued their mother because the biggest purse available was her car insurance.

continued

continued

3 **Critique the following passage using pictures. You will notice that this passage was also used in the systems chapter.**

There is a story told around the British Rolls-Royce engineering works that Boeing, the American aircraft company, once very carefully sent Rolls-Royce what you and I would describe as an aluminium drinking straw. It was about a foot (30 cm) long, with a hole down the middle about 2 millimetres in diameter, like a drinking straw. Boeing had machined this thin rod out of a block of aluminium and then drilled it down the centre. Boeing sent it to Rolls-Royce as proof of its precision engineering skill. I gather aluminium is not an easy metal to use for this sort of high-precision machining and drilling work, partly because it is hard to get a very pure sample. Drilling out the 'straw' required some very specialised vacuum chamber lathe equipment.

Rolls-Royce's version of this story was that after examining this work and admiring it, the engineers re-drilled it down the centre so as to enlarge the centre-hole diameter. They then made and slotted a smaller brass 'straw' as a lining inside the aluminium one, such that the original internal diameter of the aluminium straw was not changed. It looked like a silver straw lined with a brass straw. Then they sent it back.

4 Using Technical, Organizational and Personal Perspectives to Critique

Provide three critiques of the following passage by imagining you are:

1   a computer engineer,

2   a solicitor employed by the bank in the passage, and

3   a psychologist employed by the main character.

After that, describe the conversation that might follow if these three people were asked to work together to prioritise their concerns.

> A true story. In those early days the international banks did not invest overnight, rather using the time to allow computer operators to run the routine file backup jobs. It was a lonely and undemanding job, wandering around a deserted office block just checking the computers were doing their thing. One such operator started to occupy his nights playing a computer game pretending to invest the bank's reserves on the international money markets. He never actually signed up any contracts but did keep a record of what he would have made if he had been doing it for real; it amounted to a small fortune. For different reasons his bosses became concerned that it was unwise to have one person alone wandering about the bank unsupervised all night, so they recruited a woman to keep an eye on him. Now there were two people wandering around the bank all night with little to do. They became lovers and eventually he showed her his investment game. She suggested that he should do it for real. He did, and accumulated a real fortune. They withdrew the money and cleared off to Bermuda together.

Before commenting on the passage let me explain the choice of the three viewpoints suggested before the passage. You may be aware of various popular methods for the classification of events. Examples include dividing a problem up into the political, environmental, social and technology issues (PEST analysis), or into strengths and weaknesses, the opportunities, and threats the situation presents (SWOT analysis). This chapter presents an alternative to these, one that is really quite different. It has been carefully developed from a distillation of organisational theory, the complex problem-solving literature and the theory of knowledge. Linstone (1999), sometimes with Mitroff (Mitroff and Linstone, 1993), has suggested that solutions to complex social situations need to be critiqued from three perspectives (viewpoints):

- **technical (T),**

- **organisational (O), and**

- **personal (P).**

Simply put, tentative solutions to complex social problems need to be better appreciated by examining them from the perspective of:

- **T: an engineer (scientist),**

- **O: a managing director (politician, sociologist), and**

- **P: a psychologist (personal view).**

See Figure 4.1. These three perspectives then need to be compared and the points where they collide used as learning opportunities. A second-level learning occurs where the perspectives appear to contradict each other.

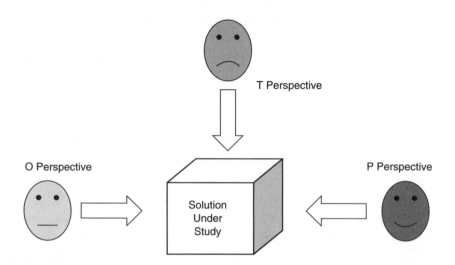

Figure 4.1   A representation of TO&P

I will now apply the TO&P critique stance to the passage above on the bank IT fraud (this is, of course my own interpretation). Let's assume someone had suggested that the chief executive of the bank be sacked.

A scientist's (T) report on the passage might ask for quantitative evidence, measurements, how much was lost compared with how much could have been lost or compared with the bank's overall resources. How did the fraud compare in dollar terms to credit card losses and so on? Is the crime big enough to warrant sacking the chief executive?

An accountant (T) may point out that nothing was actually stolen, as the operators merely invested the bank's money overnight and made an extra return. It is illegal, because of the downside risk, but the bank does not have less money. The more relevant question may be: if it is worthwhile, then why did it take the bank itself so long to appreciate the investment opportunities? Perhaps the investments manager should be sacked?

A corporate lawyer (O) responding to this passage might be concerned with legal and financial exposure by the bank. Could the bank be sued for inappropriate custodian systems to safeguard its clients' money? Could the blame be shifted to those who are responsible for the bank's computer systems? Is it worth the publicity of pursuing those who committed the fraud? Would sacking the chief executive be a public statement that the bank was being poorly managed in all areas?

A psychologist (P) might have questioned the anticipated loyalties of two people left isolated by an impersonal company. Further, the environment of boredom, in the presence of computers and bank investment accounts, may have tempted the operators to a higher level of personal risk taking. An alternative personal perspective on the passage would be to point out it was a romantic, adventurous episode in a backdrop of sterile corporate indifference. Perhaps the human resources manager should be sacked?

Consideration of the contradictions between perspectives might include consideration of how to identify the optimum balance between security and operating convenience. Was this a security failure or failure of professional trust? How can you overcome loyalties building up between colleagues that threaten to reject the needs of the employer? How can you overcome the opportunity for fraud or liability when complex specialist machinery is responsible for financial transactions?

Turning the critique process around, I would say the IT fraud passage has been written from a personal perspective (P). If it had contained a lot of statistics about IT fraud

I would have said it was written from a T or technical perspective. An organisational perspective may have discussed the design and effectiveness of management control systems in impersonal terms. Therefore, when you critique any passage you could ask yourself which perspective the author has used and how different it would look if alternative perspectives had been employed. So for example, with the IT fraud passage, if it contained a lot of statistics about fraud I would say it was written from a T perspective. If it contained a lot about organisational controls, professional ethics, trust or risk I would say it was written from an O perspective.

Why these perspectives?

First, they reflect the literature in complex problem solving. Much of this was mathematical or scientific in nature, namely operational research (T). Complex mathematical methods were suggested for dealing with complex problems such as scheduling, transportation, resource allocation and queuing. These, however, often failed to take into account human issues, or demanded too much structure in a dynamic, recursive, unstructured world. Another stream of the problem-solving literature (O) drew on sociology. Motivation and creativity seemed to be group activities. People were found to do everything better, from forecasting to athletics, when in social groups. Culture, national and organisational, was found to be more than the sum of the personalities of the individual members. This social theory became language clogged, and more descriptive than prescriptive. Norms of group behaviour were only valid when not brought to the attention of those involved. The classic case was body language which when exposed started to be used actively, making sincerity hard to judge by those trying to read other people's postures. The third thread in the complex problem-solving literature was applied psychology (P). Personality traits, cognitive styles and human information processing were tested mainly using questionnaires or a laboratory setting, often on undergraduates. Our ability to switch our psychology depending on the situation started to undermine much of this work, which was mainly empirical and thus often provided little explanation as to why we behaved as we did.

The problem-solving literature also matured from an assumption that organisational problems were like mathematical problems. One clever graduate could not appreciate and solve the problem using structured rules of calculus or logic on a computer from the safety of an office. Organisational problems and tentative solutions are socially constructed, community defined and socially appreciated, not mathematically solved. Solutions were ideological; multiple perspectives and stakeholder commitment were required. No one person owned the problem, nor could solve it. All of this shifted problem solving from mathematics as but one perspective, others coming from those affected.

The TO&P perspectives also seem to be informed by theories of knowledge. Science has long given us its rules for creating and validating new knowledge (T). It primarily involves measurement, precision, repeatability and physical objects. While excellent for many purposes, it is insufficient for learning in complex situations where issues of justice, motivation, perception, ideology, character and culture have a significant impact on identifying and solving problems. For example, science cannot decide for us if indigenous peoples should have better access to their traditional lands, or whether organisations are ethical in supplying products which do not fully reflect their sales promotion material. Knowledge of this sort cannot be measured but it can be reasonable, justified. As in a court case, the community can listen to alternative arguments and form a reasoned response (O). Then again there are many things we do because we think we know something that has never been formally justified to a sceptical audience. This personal knowledge (P) may include how creative we are or how competent at various tasks.

Linstone (1999) puts together the complex problem-solving literature and the theory of knowledge literature into his three perspectives: TO&P. Rather than rank them, or classify them against particular problem types, Linstone argues that they be used to generate three often contradictory perspectives. Learning occurs from the contradictions, and oversimplified solutions are avoided. Those involved need to construct an agreed, perhaps multiple, solution from what has been appreciated through the three perspectives. Therefore TO&P offers more than SWOT or PEST analyses in that it draws on a more socially constructed view of problems and solutions, plus it draws on a range of theories of knowledge. However, it also starts with a tentative solution and evaluates it, rather than believing the solution will emerge from the analysis. This tentative solution approach is discussed further in the chapter on decision making and reflection.

Further examples

Two well-documented organisational examples of complex social situations that have been analysed are the Space Shuttle *Challenger* disaster and the Bhopal disaster. These are very briefly critiqued below using the TO&P stance. The shuttle disaster, *Challenger*, occurred in an atmosphere of calls for the space programme to be closed down as it was costing too much money for a realistic return when many Americans were living in poverty.

An engineer's report (T) on the *Challenger* disaster found that the cause of the loss of life was that metal rings that hold the sections of the main booster rocket together cracked and broke shortly after take-off. The cold outside air temperature made them brittle.

This suggests the solution was simply to fix the small mechanical fault and then continue the programme.

In contrast, a management report (O) found that the loss of life was due to the management processes of NASA which had reached a point where it allowed the decision to launch to be dictated by concerns about public relations over engineering advice. This suggests a solution of culture change, which is long term and often hard to achieve.

A more personal-level report (P) found that the problem was that certain individuals failed to process information holistically. Consideration of the contradictions between these three perspectives might include the consideration that while public relations are important for the long-term funding of NASA, how is that to be balanced with the management of a reasonable level of operational engineering risk in a research programme? Strong personalities are often required to focus and champion organisational change projects. But, when does being a strong advocator turn into 'one-eyed' bullying? This again, however, suggests a simple solution of merely sacking problematic managers and continuing the space programme.

Further learning occurs by thinking about the contradictions generated by seeing the disaster from these three different perspectives. How can you have an organisation that epitomises scientific research (T) and evidence-based decision making, negotiating with a public relations department (O) whose main activities are entertaining community leaders, and/or advancing the idea of project champions and strong leadership (P)?

In the case of Bhopal, an explosion at a chemical manufacturing plant gassed to death many thousands of local residents. A (very brief) three-perspective analysis does reveal a more complex situation than is suggested by the tentative solution to prosecute the local chief executive. There were:

- **a mechanical failure of manufacturing plant (T),**

- **a managerial failure to respond to the root cause of safety incidents, and blindly transferring technology from the United States to India (O), and**

- **at a personal level employees did not appreciate they were dealing with anything so dangerous (P).**

The citizens of Bhopal wanted Western manufacturing technologies to boost economic development but they may not have equated well to Indian cultural strengths. So were the politicians who attracted the industry into the region as much to blame as the plant managers?

Summary

This whole book is an argument that if we look written at passages, tentative solutions or indeed any phenomenon from different viewpoints then learning occurs. If these viewpoints are insightful and rationally justified to a knowledgeable audience then new valid knowledge can be created. This particular chapter has used Linstone's division of the organisational theory literature and theories of knowledge to suggest three specific viewpoints that may be of particular use in critiquing organisational behaviour. Linstone does not restrict the number of viewpoints to three but perhaps too many would be confusing.

- **The technical (T) perspective is one of quantification, of counting and measurement.**

- **The organisational perspective (O) is one of group behaviour, social effects and systems.**

- **The personal perspective (P) is one of individuals, of their concerns, personalities, cognition and needs.**

While applying each of these to a tentative solution of a complex social situation is expected to generate a more holistic appreciation of that possible solution, further learning occurs by identifying and thinking about the contradictions, paradoxes and dilemmas generated when comparing these perspectives.

TO&P critique questions

The questions below draw on the TO&P stance of critiquing. Ask yourself the following questions about a passage, assuming a tentative solution:

- **Is the passage written from the viewpoint of measurements, organisation or individuals?**

- **How would it have been different if it were from a different perspective?**

- **Have the different perspectives of the people and/or cultures been provided?**

- **Have the people or cultural norms been treated as 'things' or as intelligent and experienced people who can inform the author?**

- **Have all stakeholders had a voice?**

- Has the author treated the problem addressed in the passage as one that can usefully be solved by using scientific methods, i.e. taken a technical perspective? If so:

  o Is the problem usefully subdivided into parts that can be measured?

  o Is the situation repeatable so the measurements can be confirmed?

  o Is it realistic to exclude any variables that have been excluded?

  o Which stakeholder is to judge the solution as valid?

  o Is the evidence provided direct, empirical or experiential?

- Has the author treated the problem addressed in the passage as best being solved by appreciating the perspectives of the stakeholders (P)? If so:

  o Do you get to hear their perspectives in their own words?

  o How were opinions justified?

  o Was the author cynical of whether the stakeholders understood their own minds or actions?

  o Was any confirming evidence sought?

  o What did stakeholders think of other stakeholders' perspectives?

- If a cultural norms perspective is being taken, is there a clear distinction between culture and personality? For example,

  o Does the author assume that the culture is more than the personality of a few dominant leaders?

  o Are the emergent properties of the culture identified and relevant?

  o How universal is the culture; are there contradictory subcultures?

Bibliography

For more on perspectival thinking see:

Wicklund (1999), Maio Makay and Metcalfe (2001), Aerts et al. (1994) and Haynes (2000).

Exercises

1 **Critique the following passage using the TO&P stance. Assume the first sentence is the tentative solution.**

There should be a monument put up to the users of early model computers. They were dreadful things to operate. I suspect those that tolerated the beasts were driven by an overwhelming desire to avoid having to deal with human beings. Life was hell for the semi-computerised storekeeper prior to the adoption of bar code readers. Imagine supermarkets and builders merchants coding every single product line. Brass screws, Size 8, 1 inch, countersunk = code 01536; Brass screw, No. 6, 2 inch, round head = code 23976 ...: every single product line needs a unique code. In those days this number had to be carefully copied from docket to docket by bored young clerks. The NATO military, having plenty of money, a love of boys' toys, and pressure for good logistics, were often leaders in this sort of technology. They had sixteen-digit codes to identify parts such as the lens for a certain type of camera, that fitted a certain range of aircraft, designed differently (but compatible) by different NATO countries, to a certain operational specifications which varied over time. Despite the presence of check digits, there was real concern that one day a storekeeper expecting delivery of a small package containing a specific replacement camera lens would instead receive a fully armed tank.

2 **Critique the following passage using the TO&P stance. Assume the tentative solution is that the senior officers responsible for the practice should be imprisoned for cruelty to special forces soldiers.**

During the Malay campaign in the 1950s British special forces soldiers were posted one per village all over the parts of Malay where it was thought communists were likely to be operating. The villagers tended to be anti-communist so allowed the soldiers to maintain radio contact with army intelligence on a daily basis. If no call came, or the wrong call sign was given, then it was assumed that the communists had overrun the village. This gave those sitting comfortably in headquarters a very convenient overall map of where the communists were. I gather the soldiers were trained for this work on the basis that if the communists came to a village they should clear off, and go bush. The soldiers then had to make their own way home, often through very rugged jungle. There were pictures of some very thin-looking soldiers as they staggered home. It meant that the soldiers had first to be given some very extensive jungle survival training. The part of this training that caught my childish eye was the daily breakfast of snake. The soldiers had to start the day by selecting a snake from a tank, kill it, skin it and then eat it raw. I don't know if this was really effective training but whenever I now

continued

continued

watch people select live lobsters from a water tank, or people in the Australian bush eating grubs, I think of the snake breakfasts and the acts of those now largely forgotten soldiers.

3 **Critique the following passage using the TO&P stance. This passage was also used in the systems chapter. Assume the tentative claim that orphan lambs should be put down.**

We rented a farmhouse from a wonderful man, Ron, who farmed sheep in New Zealand. When my young daughters saw newborn lambs wandering about his farm bleating for their mothers they asked him if they could feed them, make them pets. Quite rightly he pointed out that if they did that when the lamb and mother were in a good relationship they could be responsible for the mother rejecting her own lamb. However, there was often a lamb or two whose mother died and he would find one for them to care for. Many of these orphan lambs died despite all good intentions, either because they also turned out to be very weak after the birth or because they had failed to get that crucial first feed from their mother. I gather this sets up the stomach of the lamb. However, a little later in life these pet lambs face yet another risk because a few months of being hand-fed by humans scrambles their survival instincts. Untamed sheep know to run away from people. Pet lambs know the opposite. They run towards people who call out to them, thinking there is a free feed about. So, some less-than-desirable people know that if they are driving past a mob of sheep and fancy a feed it was well worth just standing at the edge of a paddock and calling out. The non-pet lambs run away but the pet lambs run towards whoever is shouting. When close enough they got banged on the head and quickly thrown into the car boot.

Using Concern Solving to Critique

Critique the following:

The problem of the car not starting was solved by shooting the car's owner.

Murder aside, does this action actually solve the problem of the car not starting? The car still does not start. Why would anyone think that it does? Anyway, who said it was a problem, and who says it is solved? With the owner dead does anyone else now want to point out that the car will not start?

An *objective* view of this problem of the car not starting is that it is an 'out there' problem, independent of who looks at it, independent of any particular human mind, a universal problem. It exists regardless of the presence of any human being. Any rational person would agree that the car is not starting; they can test it for themselves. The problem will not be fixed until everyone agrees that the car can be started.

A *subjective* view of this problem is that an inanimate car itself cannot and does not know or care if it starts. It does not have a problem; it has not identified a gap between what it wants and what it has. Nothing inanimate can sense that a problem exists. Likewise, if our planet was overrun with very large green ants then it would not be concerned; it cannot feel that there is a problem. For a problem to exist then there has to be a concerned person present, a subjective. This raises the possibility of solving problems by removing the concerned person or, less dramatically, changing their concerns. Problems are socially constructed, so solutions must include changing people's concerns.

Definition

Wilson (1983) defines concern as 'a readiness to exert influence: a readiness to act'. A failure to be able to act often heightens concern. Keen (2000) talks about exploring communities' concerns rather than identifying 'topics' when trying to understand them. Dewey (Argyris and Schon, 1978) uses the term 'doubts' as the driver for human activity. These terms are similar, in concept, to how the word 'concern' is being used here, as is Habermas's term 'cognitive interests' quoted in Ulrich (1983).

It would seem reasonable to classify concerns into two groups, those from nature (instinctive) and those from nurture (communicated). For primal survival concerns, language is not thought paramount. For instance, small children instinctively know to stay away from rows of sharp teeth and cliff edges whereas concerns over being burnt may be learnt either from touching a fire or from observing the panic-like actions of parents. More complex concerns, such as promotion at work, are socially constructed through dialogue later in life. Barnes and Bloor (1982) argue that humans not only have (like all species) instinctive concerns, but uniquely appear to have a concern anticipation and concern-solving disposition. We humans seem to have an environmental competitive advantage in our desire, supported by our language skills, to create and solve concerns of our own perception. For example, NASA scientists are exploring for water (oxygen and hydrogen) on planets to allow the building of life support systems and for rocket fuel. Is there a problem here that 'needs' to be solved, or is the real driver merely curiosity, or threat anticipation? Extreme sports are another example: in this case, solving the problem of how to get a safe thrill. If dealing with threats is seen as concern solving, the evolutionary advantage becomes clearer. Those humans who have avoided death by anticipating threats may have produced more offspring. Technological advancement itself can be seen as overcoming basic human concerns about controlling nature and food resources.

Cognitive authority

Wilson (1983) uses the term 'cognitive authority' to describe those people who influence our concerns. In the media literature this is called 'agenda setting' (Liebl, 2002). Influencing people's concerns may act to alter their information wants. Persuasion is really about altering people's concerns, a practice well versed in advertising. Managing an organisational problem from appreciation to solution can be perceived as being really about managing people's concerns. This will include appreciating those concerns, trying to clarify them, trying to satisfy them, and trying to alter them. Put another way, managers and specialists can act to alter the perceptions of those involved in the problem, which, in turn, affects their concerns.

Problem solving

Landry (1995) tracks the history of operational research criticising it for an overemphasis on the objective view of organisational problems, which he claims leads to viewing problems as being 'like an island' that anyone can circumnavigate and there-fore understand. He also calls for more appreciation of the fact that problems are per-ceptions in people's minds. Therefore solutions require changing those perceptions, sometimes by altering the performance of the object of the perception and sometimes by redirecting the perception. These perceptions are perhaps determined by concerns. However, some seven years later Liebl, in the same discipline, calls for a change from the word 'problem' to that of 'issues', so as to align with societal problems. While the term 'issues' still fails to subjectify problems, Liebl does at least provide an extensive review of issues that could be aligned with 'concerns'. Moreover he discusses ideas such as whether concerns have life cycles. This life cycle view is attractive in that many con-cerns can be imagined to be born, grow and eventually die down. However, this 'life' metaphor plays down the 'agenda-setting' possibilities of persuasive groups who can manufacture our concerns.

Information

Taking a more functional information processing approach, Metcalfe and Powell (1995) argue that it is people's concerns (real interests) that they use to interpret the millions of messages they constantly receive from the environment. Metcalfe and Powell believe that these 'concerns' are the primary lens for selecting information from 'everything going on out there', the idea being that, if you are concerned about some-thing, this 'determines' your priorities to these messages. Put another way, your personal ethics or values act to interpret how you evaluate the world, so concerns and values (and ethics) appear to be linked, and provide perspectives on life and its problems.

Polanyi (1966), while defining tacit knowledge, argues that experience will change a person's concerns over a problem. In other words, an experienced person will have different concerns over a *problem* than an inexperienced one. Learning from the expe-rienced, therefore, involves the inexperienced trying to understand the difference between their concerns as compared with the concerns of the experienced.

The identification of the problem in a passage followed by the distinction between problems and concerns can be used to critique, to provide a different view of the pas-sage by switching from an objective to a subjective view of the problem (concern). Critique the following passage using the stance of switching from seeing a problem to one of seeing concerned persons or the other way around.

There is a wonderful system of public footpaths throughout England. These give non-landowners the opportunity to romp through the countryside getting exercise, fresh air and a chance to admire England's wonderful scenery. Some of these pathways were established as legal public rights of way only after hard-fought political battles. Prior to the proclamation of a new footpath campaigners would often walk along the proposed routes to see what reaction they got from the landowners. There is a tale about one rather strong-willed walker bumping into an irate landowner. The quarrel went something like this:

'Get off my land.'
'What makes all this huge moorland only yours?'
'It was given to my forefathers by the King of England.'
'Why?' asked the walker.
'For fighting alongside the king against the French at the Battle of Agincourt in 1415.'
To which came the retort from the walker:
'That sounds fair enough, mate. Take your jacket off and I'll fight you for it now.'

The problem in this passage seems to be that of landownership, or at least right of way across land. As an impersonal problem it is one of appropriate legislation. If the land transfer from the king to the 'noble' was or is now legal, then the walkers need legislation that gives them the right to pass. Law that allows access to others to freehold land is commonplace. In most countries, emergency services and utilities as well as mineral exploration staff are allowed access as they require.

The humour in the passage comes from its taking a personal view rather than a legal one. However, thinking about the *concerns* of all the participants in the story brings out a slightly different critique. Using the concerns stance my critique of this passage is that it is a personal view that depicts a contradiction in concerns between the landowner and the walker:

- **The landowner is concerned about litter, erosion, damage, gates left open, lack of privacy, legal liability if an accident occurs on his property and the erosion of his privilege as the owner of land.**

- **The walker is concerned for his access to beautiful things, and his health.**

The walker may also be concerned about the inherited privilege, and an ideology that allows for a very unequal distribution of wealth based on birthright rather than public service. If he did the same as the landowner in terms of risking his life in battle, as many common soldiers do every day, then they all would still not become the owners of large expanses of land.

Try this next passage. Identify the problem, the participants and their apparent concerns.

That cities are extremely effective in developing creativity, culture and wealth is not in doubt. The clustering of diverse ideas seems to generate more ideas. Ironically, though, this intense clustering of city dwellers requires the establishment of an inordinate number of rules of behaviour. I suspect that these are the clouds that accompany silver linings. There are rules for everything: where you can park you car, how to use non-gendered language, when you can shout, what colour you can paint your house, whether you can change the shape of your garage, how to drive your car, etc., *ad nauseam* – there are rules, rules everywhere. Some people love these rules; they want more signs reminding you of the rules and to chair committees making up new rules. Rule makers rule community organisations so when we ask them what we can do to improve the world, they suggest more rules. I saw this paradox between creativity and rules play out one winter's morning while driving home on a busy three-lane freeway. It was a very clear, cold and black ice morning. I came to a hill on the freeway which was only as steep as hills on freeways tend to be. As vehicles, mainly trucks, tried to drive up the hill their wheels spun on the black ice bringing them to a near stand-still, not skidding sideways, just slowing to a crawl, but unlikely to make it to the top of the hill for some considerable time. As more vehicles arrived, the three lanes became filled with cars with spinning wheels. It was like a traffic jam for no reason. The normal rules no longer applied. One or two people quickly realised the situation and broke the rule about crossing the middle strip. Others turned around and used the breakdown lane to go back to a nearby on-ramp. Before long the police arrived and started punishing these creative drivers for breaking the rules.

Using the objective view that things can have problems, like cars not starting, this passage suggests at least two problems to me:

1 **That cities need rules, and yet need to be creative.**

2 **That ice on a freeway is a very real danger to road users.**

Critiquing the passage in this way suggests that a solution to the first problem is to propose a process in the making of new rules where they have to be vetted by a creativity committee whose job is to ensure they do not stifle creativity. I do not have high hopes for this committee being very effective. The ice problem might be solved simply by improving the freeway maintenance programme, including requiring those responsible to be more aware of weather forecasts and provide a weather response plan, perhaps in the form of spreading grit on the roads.

A subjective view of this passage, that problems are really individuals' personal concerns, makes me see the passage slightly differently, and perhaps in terms of developing citizens' appreciations rather than offer solutions. Who, apart from me, is even aware of the issue of the creativity inherent in cities? I assume this creativity comes in the form of culture, philosophy and economics. The last means creativity in products and services. So, a concerns perspective would make me want to ask the citizens if they see living in the city as an opportunity for creativity and how they might want to improve things. I would also want to know if they feel oppressed or saved by the numerous rules that accompany living in a city. This might have to be undertaken as a comparison with living in the country. However, if they do not think there is a problem, then there is no problem. Who am I to impose my views on others?

Summary

This chapter has suggested a means of critiquing that involves moving between an objective and subjective view of problems. An objective view sees problems as independent of the presence of any particular concerned person. A subjective view involves identifying who is concerned, who has the problem, and trying to alter those concerns. For example, in the traffic passage the police have concerns over traffic violations. If they were to agree that special circumstances existed then they would not have a problem with the motorists' actions. For more on concern solving or real interests see Habermas (1968).

Critique questions

Ask yourself the following questions about the passage:

- **What is the problem revealed by the passage?**

- **Are there other problems?**

- **Are the problems inter-related?**

- **How could the problems be solved?**

- **Who are the people in the passage (include the author and yourself)?**

- **What are their concerns?**

- **Are their concerns personal, technical or organisational?**

- **How might these concerns be alleviated?**

Exercises

1 **Identify the problem(s) in the following passage and then identify the concerns. Suggest solutions.**

I spent fifteen years of my life as a university lecturer; it beats working for a living. It was the endless repetition of untested myths that got to me, not the seven-hour weeks. One lasting concern I have of mass education, private or public, is the arrogance of teachers which leads to their trying to dominate the student's thinking processes. When the teacher is knowledgeable and competent this is not too much of a problem, but when the teacher has not fully matured it is. The less mature teachers do not appreciate the morality also being taught in their everyday rambling. For example, science is about exploiting natural resources; accounting unquestionably places capital before labour. A slightly more explicit form of this happened to my children when at primary school in New Zealand. I was surprised when jokingly I asked my 7-year-old daughter what God looks like. She responded confidently by asking which God I was talking about. The god of the sea or the god of the hills? To a WASP (ex-Protestant) like me this reply was a bit confusing. The competitive advantage of the God I heard about as a child was that he was The God, the One God. God of everything and everywhere, you could not escape even after death. What had happened was the New Zealand government had decreed that primary school children would be taught Maori. A great move. However, there was another rule that said religion would not be taught until the kids were a bit older and even then it would be an elective. In practice this meant preaching from Jesus's supporters rather than from religious historians or philosophers. As Maori language and culture includes its religion, the kids were hearing about the Maori gods before they heard about Adam and Eve, Jesus and the One God story. When my daughter was eventually taught about the Old Testament she found it less convincing than the Maori version.

2 **Identify the problem(s) in the following passage and then identify the concerns. Suggest solutions.**

You may have noticed how many people are in the habit of blaming others for any misfortune that befalls them. A lesser example is blaming teachers for not teaching them, while the extreme example is, 'I killed him because my mother mistreated me.' Taking responsibility for our own actions and the outcomes we achieve is in danger with excess doses of welfare states and sociology. Sports people are as guilty as any. Reporters rush up to athletes and ask them why they did not win. A whole list of rather unconvincing excuses comes back, often involving a

continued

continued

biased referee. I was impressed by the stand made by an Australian male swimmer in the 1990 Commonwealth Games. He came second and a very nationalistic reporter asked why. The swimmer answered by saying, 'Because I swam slower than the person that came first.' The reporter persisted, 'But wasn't there some problems of back pressure in your lane?' The swimmer repeated, 'I don't know about that but I do know that my turns could be improved.' It was such a pleasant change to hear someone take responsibility for themselves.

3   **Identify the problem(s) in the following passage and then identify the concerns. Suggest solutions. This passage was used in the TO&P chapter.**

A true story. In those early days the international banks did not invest overnight, rather using the time to allow computer operators to run the routine file backup jobs. It was a lonely and undemanding job, wandering around a deserted office block just checking the computers were doing their thing. One such operator started to occupy his nights playing a computer game pretending to invest the bank's reserves on the international money markets. He never actually signed up any contracts but did keep a record of what he would have made if he had been doing it for real; it amounted to a small fortune. For different reasons his bosses became concerned that it was unwise to have one person alone wandering about the bank unsupervised all night, so they recruited a woman to keep an eye on him. Now there were two people wandering around the bank all night with little to do. They became lovers and eventually he showed her his investment game. She suggested that he should do it for real. He did, and accumulated a real fortune. They withdrew the money and cleared off to Bermuda together.

6 Using Observation and Explanation to Critique

Critique the following passage in terms of how effective observations were in terms of solving the problem. Was it worth undertaking any empirical measurements to prove a point? Why do the balls hit the ground at the same time?

Many years ago and after many hours of rolling cannon balls down inclined planes, Galileo got into a dispute with his fellow lecturers. They were lecturing to their students that if two weights were dropped from a height the heaviest would hit the ground first. Galileo disagreed, so they decided to conduct an experiment to decide the matter. They went to the top of the Leaning Tower of Pisa and started dropping cannon balls over the top balcony in twos, one large and one small. Unfortunately an argument started about exactly how to line up the two balls at their starting position and how to be sure both were released at exactly the same time. The landing was also hard to measure. Some preliminary trials soon revealed you need some very accurate measuring devices to be able to detect which ball actually did hit the ground first. Moreover, the lighter ball appeared to move faster to start with but then the heavy one tended to catch up. Observation was (as ever) proving to raise more questions than it solved. Galileo then came up with a thought experiment. He reasoned that if a large cannon ball and a small one were melted together into a larger cannon ball then his ball would have the average speed of the original balls. Now if you dropped all three, the new largest ball cannot fall the fastest because it is the average speed of the other two; however, it is the largest ball so should fall the fastest. This dilemma is only solved if all three balls hit the ground together.

History

Before critiquing this passage, some background on the use of observation and explanation to solve problems may be helpful. Over the last few hundred years science has emerged from religion, the Enlightenment, defining itself by observation and measurement. Science was only those physical things you could observe and measure, while religion was about those things you could not, the spiritual world. The root metaphor of science is 'seeing' as in 'insightful' and 'seeing is believing'. Doubting Thomas in the Gospels has the scientific attitude; he wanted to see before he would believe. Religion's root metaphor is feelings. Scientists therefore see problem solving (research, enquiry) as collecting data through the senses, through empirics. It was not just seeing (observation) but use of any of the senses – hearing, touch, smell and taste. Spiritual problems were declared non-scientific because they could not be tested using the senses, through empirics.

Unreliable senses

Everyday experience is problem solving through the senses so was originally thought to be scientific. However, concerns over how easily humans are deceived by their senses started to arise. Anyone who watches television knows you cannot always trust your senses. Figure 6.1 contains some classic examples provided by the human information processing literature (Kahneman et al., 1982 and http:// www.scientificpsychic.com/graphics/).

This problem of the senses easily being deceived was countered by the philosophy of science writers with a call for empirics (observation, smell, etc.) to be repeatable, in front of a sceptical audience. See for yourself. Thus the repeatable laboratory experiment became the hallmark of the scientist. This also allows for the observation to be repeated using the impressive reasoning power of 'if–then' logic. For example, an experiment could be set up to solve the problem that:

> *if* salt is mixed with water *then* its volume will increase.

This could be changed to:

> if sugar is added to water then its volume will increase, or if sand is added to water its volume will not increase, and so on.

This allows for a process of elimination, a reduction of the phenomenon observed to specific situations. The problem of salt added to water not increasing its volume is to be solved using observation and 'if–then' logic.

Explanation why

However, as you may have realised, unless there is some sort of explanation (theory) of *why* the results are not as expected, then the learning process is somewhat unsatisfactory. The philosopher Immanuel Kant (1724–1804) pointed this out. Using a different example, why

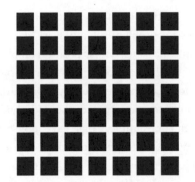

There are no grey dots between the squares.

The shade of grey of each circle is the same, only the background alters.

All the lines are parallel.

Figure 6.1 Optical illustions. Reproduced with permission of Antonio Zamora (www.scientificpsychic.com/graphics/index.html; accessed 19 October 2005).

do people bang the side of their television when it is not working properly? If they answer 'I do not know' or '*because* it works' then this is rather unconvincing, unscientific – there is no explanation. I can observe someone's behaviour but without explanation of why they acted in a certain way I cannot judge how to respond. Explanation without observation is incomplete; they are a joined pair. By explanation it is meant 'why' something occurs; it is often called 'a theory'[3] and flagged using the word 'because'.

Some researchers, typically critical social theorists, prefer to focus on the explanations rather than the observations for problem solving. Karl Marx, whose ideas have improved the lives of millions of people, has a particular position on observation (Sowell, 1985) as a means of solving problems. While Marx called his work empirical (using sensory data), he was not just interested in the 'mere appearance' of things. Rather, he thought it was important to understand why an observation existed, the underlying 'processes in tension' that cause an appearance to occur. For example, a married couple can be living, eating and sleeping together but not be happy with their relationship. The appearance is of a compatible couple, but really to understand marriage you need to understand the underlying tensions that result in the state of marriage. Mere observation of the relationship might not reveal very much. Marx used the example of the caterpillar. You cannot really understand the caterpillar by merely observing and measuring it. You need also to understand the underlying evolutionary forces driving its life cycle. What appears in the physical form for us to observe is the result of some underlying forces. A small change in these and what we observe can change significantly. Environmentalists know this only too well through the example of the introduction of species into new habitats. Therefore, critical theorists concern themselves more about the 'why' explanation than the observation, and the 'why' is often analysed in term of underlying tensions, contradictions. This lack of centrality of observation to problem solving can also be found in some areas of science. Einstein's work was mainly mathematical and thought experiments. Observational experiments on his explanations of how the physical world worked were not possible until space travel. His classic book *Relativity*, however, draws almost exclusively on thought experiments or analogies from personal experience to ask the reader to imagine what was happening.

In a circular manner, it also appears that having a prior explanation for something affects what we observe, or at least how we interpret what we see. Using an example from the first chapter, if someone has a lot of experience of uncontrolled dogs attacking passers-by, then they will intuitively interpret the sight of a dog tied to a post differently to someone who has extensive experience of dogs being mistreated. The experience stored in our brains intuitively *explains* what we 'see'. Indeed our prior explanations seem to bring to our notice details from a broad picture. So, if you are walking down a busy road, what details you notice in that broad picture and how you react is most likely determined by your own prior explanations of what is before you.

Empirics as experience

The American pragmatic (James, 1907/1910) approach to observation seems to be slightly different again from the scientific view of observation as simply being the source of valid knowledge. It sees observations more as a stimulation to help people think through explanations of what is happening around them. Observation causes an experience, an intuitive response which can be reflected upon so we can better understand our thinking processes. The emphasis is not on seeking independent objective observations but on improving our reasoning and our understanding of how thinking occurs. Act, try something, and learn what happens. It is pragmatic knowledge that is gained if what is done changes what is seen. Observation of the changes caused by an action enables learning. Explanations of the world come from observing what happens when changes are enacted. Pragmatism suggests a more active form of observation. We understand our situation from observing the effect of our actions (changes, intervention). Designing learning loops from intervention in the situation replaces independent observation as the source of valid knowledge. This makes pragmatism perhaps more relevant to complex social situations (like organisational change) than scientific empiricism. Moreover, it advocates learning from a series of small trial and error learning loops rather than 'one big' experiment.

This discussion about observation now needs to be applied as a critique stance on the cannon balls passage. Observation was originally intended to resolve an argument because it is repeatable, which provides a very strong type of evidence. However, the argument moved from that of the relative speed of the balls to that of how to measure the observations. Rather than become a source of valid knowledge the measurement problems became 'noise' to be eliminated. Eventually the argument was solved to the satisfaction of those present, if not to modern scientists, using reasoning in the form of a thought experiment. Even though reasoning through language rather than observation was used as evidence, those present are able to say they were being 'scientific', not spiritual. They were concerned with the physical, measurable world and used scientific means (reasoning) to solve the argument. If reasoning is merely language why does that make them scientists rather than theologians? Perhaps because they were considering physical objects and using experience (old observations) to reason. Moreover, reasoning is also fairly convincing repeatable evidence: the reasons can be repeated.

The passage also provides some small evidence of learning loops or learning from observation occurring. The numerous trials of releasing the balls taught those present that releasing the balls was an interesting physiological issue in its own right. The muscles in the hand gripped the large ball harder, making release a matter of needing to allow for relaxing that hand differently than the hand with the small ball. However, there was no evidence in the passage that those present reflected on what they had learnt from the observation attempt. Rather, the explanations were imagined before the experiment and a failure of the experiment seems to have had no impact on changing their prior explanations that size determined speed. At a different level of analysis the passage is not accurately describing an actual historical event; it is a fable. However, perhaps it does not really matter if the events described could have happened. It is drawing on the reader's experiences, using analogies to reason that the weight of the ball is (almost) irrelevant in determining its speed.

Serious Galileo

The passage below has the same hero, but this is a historical account of Galileo's classic scientific experiment as recorded by Galileo. He reports observing bronze balls rolling on an inclined plane. It seemed counter-intuitive to him that the heavy ball did not roll faster than the small ball. Note how the father of experimental science has created an opportunity for repeatable observations under controlled conditions. If only such simplicity was possible in observing human and group behaviours.

A piece of wooden moulding or scantling, about 12 cubits long, half a cubit wide, and three finger-breadths thick, was taken; on its edge was cut a channel a little more than one finger in breadth; having made this groove very straight, smooth, and polished, and having lined it with parchment, also as smooth and polished as possible, we rolled along it a hard, smooth, and very round bronze ball. Having placed this board in a sloping position, by raising one end some one or two cubits above the other, we rolled the ball, as I was just saying, along the channel, noting, in a manner presently to be described, the time required to make the descent. We repeated this experiment more than once in order to measure the time with an accuracy such that the deviation between two observations never exceeded one-tenth of a pulse-beat. Having performed this operation and having assured ourselves of its reliability, we now rolled the ball only one-quarter the length of the channel; and having measured the time of its descent, we found it precisely one-half of the former. Next we tried other distances, compared the time for the whole length with that for the half, or with that for two-thirds, or three-fourths, or indeed for any fraction; in such experiments, repeated a full hundred times, we always found that the spaces traversed were to each other as the squares of the times, and this was true for all inclinations of the plane, i.e., of the channel, along which we rolled the ball. We also observed that the times of descent, for various inclinations of the plane, bore to one another precisely that ratio which, as we shall see later, the Author had predicted and demonstrated for them.

For the measurement of time, we employed a large vessel of water placed in an elevated position; to the bottom of this vessel was soldered a pipe of small diameter giving a thin jet of water which we collected in a small glass during the time of each descent, whether for the whole length of the channel or for part of its length; the water thus collected was weighed, after each descent, on a very accurate balance; the differences and ratios of these weights gave us the differences and ratios of the times, and this with such accuracy that although the operation was repeated many, many times, there was no appreciable discrepancy in the results.

Source: Galileo's (1564–1642) Acceleration Experiment as he wrote it up in *Two New Sciences*, Galilei (2001), p. 178

What is your critique of Galileo's experiment passage? Mine is first to note that it reads a little like my high school physics experiment write-ups. The diagram is missing, and I know phrases like 'the operation was repeated many, many times' would be marked down. But the passage is all about precision, accuracy and repeatability. What Galileo has measured is a fact, valid knowledge. A ball will accelerate uniformly down any such slope. His description invites anyone to repeat what he is doing, he repeats findings to ensure accuracy, but he also repeats findings in different situations. These different situations include the ball in different places on the slope and using different slopes. I do not detect any explicit attempts at falsification. Does he try and disprove what he is finding?

What is missing from the passage, to make it meaningful, are some alternative explanations. Why is he rolling a ball down a slope, why did he use the design he has, why does the ball always reach the one-quarter point in half the time and why does the ball roll down the slope in a constant ratio between the steepness of the slope and the speed? Newton's laws of motion are an explanation but did Einstein's theory of relativity supersede them?

In terms of observations needed to be explained in terms of 'underlying tensions' a critique might look to the tension suggested in the passage. This requires some knowledge of the history of Galileo's work. In recent times there has been some doubt that Galileo actually undertook some of the experiments he claims he did. If he did not do this experiment then this detailed write-up becomes a testament to how important accurate observations were to establishing valid claims of scientific knowledge. The underlying tensions for Galileo's experiments are two, if not three, fold. First he was trying to disprove some of Aristotle's explanations about physical motion, and he was defining science as separate from religion by attempting to explain only those things that could be physically observed. It is possible that these experiments were performed after Galileo was reprimanded by the Catholic Church for not proving his claim that the sun went around the earth. Further tensions of the need for accuracy and to focus on science that did not threaten the Church may be present.

In contrast the passage below was selected because it places more emphasis on observing as learning loops.

Dear Sir,

I am writing in response to your request for additional information in Box #3 of the accident report form where I put 'Poor Planning' as the cause of my accident. I trust the following details will be sufficient. I am a bricklayer by trade. On the day of the accident, I was working alone on the roof of a new six-story building. When

(Continued)

(Continued)

I completed my work, I found I had some bricks left over which, when weighed later, were found to weigh 240 lbs. Rather than carry the bricks down by hand, I decided to lower them in a barrel by using a pulley which was attached to the side of the building at the sixth floor. Securing the rope at ground level, I went up to the roof, swung the barrel out, and loaded the bricks into it. Then I went down and untied the rope, holding it tightly to ensure a slow descent of the 240 lbs of bricks. You will note on the accident reporting form that my weight is 135 lbs. Due to my surprise at being jerked off the ground so suddenly, I lost my presence of mind and forgot to let go of the rope. Needless to say, I proceeded at a rapid rate up the side of the building. In the vicinity of the third floor, I met the barrel which was now proceeding downward at an equally impressive speed. This explains the fractured skull, minor abrasions, and the broken collarbone, as listed in Section 3 of the accident reporting form. Slowed only slightly, I continued my rapid ascent, not stopping until the fingers of my right hand were two knuckles deep into the pulley which I mentioned in Paragraph 2 of this correspondence. Fortunately, by this time I had regained my presence of mind and was able to hold tightly to the rope, in spite of the excruciating pain I was now beginning to experience. At approximately the same time, however, the barrel of bricks hit the ground and the bottom fell out of the barrel. Now devoid of the weight of the bricks, the barrel weighed approximately 50 lbs. I refer you again to my weight. As you might imagine, I began a rapid descent down the side of the building. In the vicinity of the third floor, I met the barrel coming up. This accounts for the two fractured ankles, broken tooth and severe lacerations of my legs and lower body. Here my luck began to change slightly. The encounter with the barrel seemed to slow me enough to lessen my injuries when I fell into the pile of bricks and fortunately only three vertebrae were cracked. I am sorry to report, however, as I lay there on the pile of bricks, in pain, unable to move and watching the empty barrel six stories above me, I again lost my composure and presence of mind and let go of the rope.

Source: based on Gerard Hoffnung's 'The Bricklayer's Lament'; see *Hoffnung: A Last Encore, BBC Radio Collection*, BBC Books)

Observation without learning also seems inadequate.

Summary

What is valid knowledge has been critiqued by scientists using a stance that almost defines science, observation. Later, observations had to be explained, or used to justify explanations, if they were to be 'scientific' rather than religious, hearsay or mere opinion. This historically significant critique stance was introduced and applied to a series of 'experiments' whose historical accuracy might be questioned. Observation and explanation were seen as

(1) how to validate knowledge, (2) as a source for thinking about underlying tensions, and (3) how to generate idea from action (doing). For more on this see Hanson (1971).

Observational and explanation questions

To critique using the observation and explanation stance, ask yourself the following questions:

- Does the passage intend to report actual, real observations?

- Are the observations convincing? Will they alter your behaviour in any way in the future?

- Does the passage require you to use your memory; why?

- Can you infer something the writer did not infer from the same observations?

- Are the observations repeatable; does that matter?

- Are the observations generalisable to many other situations; do they remain valid across time and universally around the world?

- Were the actions that produced the observations seen as an exercise in learning from action?

- Was there any attempt at learning from a series of act–observe–reflect–act loops in the observations?

- What do the observations explain?

- What actions are to be observed in the passage and why?

Exercises

1   Critique the following passage in terms of observation and explanation. Notice the possible learning loops involved in the story.

continued

continued

FROM: Patty Lewis, Human Resources Director

TO: All Employees

DATE: October 01, 2003

RE: Christmas Party

I'm happy to inform you that the company Christmas Party will take place on December 23, starting at noon in the private function room at the Grill House. There will be a cash bar and plenty of drinks! We'll have a small band playing traditional carols … feel free to sing along. And don't be surprised if our CEO shows up dressed as Santa Claus! A Christmas tree will be lit at 1:00pm. Exchange of gifts among employees can be done at that time; however, no gift should be over $10.00 to make the giving of gifts easy for everyone's pockets. This gathering is only for employees! Our CEO will make a special announcement at that time!

Merry Christmas to you and your family.

Patty

- -

FROM: Patty Lewis, Human Resources Director

TO: All Employees

DATE: October 02, 2003

RE: Holiday Party

In no way was yesterday's memo intended to exclude our Jewish employees. We recognize that Chanukkah is an important holiday, which often coincides with Christmas, though unfortunately not this year. However, from now on we're calling it our 'Holiday Party.' The same policy applies to any other employees who are not Christians or those still celebrating Reconciliation Day. There will be no Christmas tree present. No Christmas carols sung. We will have other types of music for your enjoyment.

Happy now?

Happy Holidays to you and your family.

Patty

- -

FROM: Patty Lewis, Human Resources Director

TO: All Employees

DATE: October 03, 2003

RE: Holiday Party

Regarding the note I received from a member of Alcoholics Anonymous requesting a non-drinking table ... you didn't sign your name. I'm happy to accommodate this request, but if I put a sign on a table that reads, 'AA Only' you wouldn't be anonymous anymore. How am I supposed to handle this? Somebody?

Forget about the gifts exchange, no gifts exchange are allowed since the union members feel that $10.00 is too much money and executives believe $10.00 is a little chintzy.

NO GIFTS EXCHANGE WILL BE ALLOWED.

FROM: Patty Lewis, Human Resources Director

To: All Employees

DATE: October 04, 2003

RE: Holiday Party

What a diverse group we are! I had no idea that December 20 begins the Muslim holy month of Ramadan, which forbids eating and drinking during daylight hours. There goes the party! Seriously, we can appreciate how a luncheon at this time of year does not accommodate our Muslim employees' beliefs. Perhaps the Grill House can hold off on serving your meal until the end of the party – or else package everything for you to take it home in a little foil doggy baggy. Will that work? Meanwhile, I've arranged for members of Weight Watchers to sit farthest from the dessert buffet and pregnant women will get the table closest to the restrooms. Gays are allowed to sit with each other. Lesbians do not have to sit with Gay men, each will have their own table. Yes, there will be a flower arrangement for the Gay men's table. To the person asking permission to cross-dress, no cross-dressing

continued

continued

allowed though. We will have booster seats for short people. Low-fat food will be available for those on a diet. We cannot control the salt used in the food, we suggest for those people with high blood pressure to taste first. There will be fresh fruits as dessert for diabetics, the restaurant cannot supply 'No Sugar' desserts. Sorry!

Did I miss anything?!?!?

Patty

—————————————————————————————————

FROM: Patty Lewis, Human Resources Director

TO: All !@#&* Employees

DATE: October 05, 2003

RE: The !@#&* Holiday Party

Vegetarian pricks I've had it with you people!!! We're going to keep this party at the Grill House whether you like it or not, so you can sit quietly at the table furthest from the 'grill of death,' as you so quaintly put it, and you'll get your !@#&* salad bar, including organic tomatoes. But you know, tomatoes have feelings, too. They scream when you slice them. I've heard them scream. I'm hearing them scream right NOW! I hope you all have a rotten holiday! Drive drunk and die,

The Witch from HELL!!!!!!!!

—————————————————————————————————

FROM: Joan Bishop, Acting Human Resources Director

DATE: October 06, 2003

RE: Patty Lewis and Holiday Party

I'm sure I speak for all of us in wishing Patty Lewis a speedy recovery and I'll continue to forward your cards to her. In the meantime, management has decided to cancel our Holiday Party and give everyone the afternoon of the 23rd off with full pay.

Happy Holidays!

Thanks, Joan Bishop

(Source: unknown)

2   **Critique the following passage in terms of observation and explanation. Notice the possible learning loops involved in the story.**

A minute later we were both in a hansom, driving furiously for the Brixton Road …

    'You don't seem to give much thought to the matter in hand,' I said at last, interrupting Holmes …

    'No data yet,' he answered. 'It is a capital mistake to theorize before you have all the evidence. It biases the judgment.'

    'You will have your data soon,' I remarked, pointing with my finger; 'this is the Brixton Road, and that is the house, if I am not very much mistaken.'

    'So it is. Stop, driver, stop!' We were still a hundred yards or so from it, but he insisted upon our alighting, and we finished our journey upon foot …

    I had imagined that Sherlock Holmes would at once have hurried into the house and plunged into a study of the mystery. Nothing appeared to be further from his intention. With an air of nonchalance which, under the circumstances, seemed to me to border upon affectation, he lounged up and down the pavement, and gazed vacantly at the ground, the sky, the opposite houses and the line of railings. Having finished his scrutiny, he proceeded slowly down the path, or rather down the fringe of grass which flanked the path, keeping his eyes riveted upon the ground. Twice he stopped, and once I saw him smile, and heard him utter an exclamation of satisfaction. There were many marks of footsteps upon the wet clayey soil; but since the police had been coming and going over it, I was unable to see how my companion could hope to learn anything from it. Still I had had such extraordinary evidence of the quickness of his perceptive faculties, that I had no doubt that he could see a great deal which was hidden from me.

Source: extracts from *A Study In Scarlet*
by Arthur Conan Doyle, 1887)

continued

continued

3   Critique the passage below in terms of observation and explanation.

I imagine being on an old rusty cargo ship steaming alone through the moonlight night, mid Pacific, with all the crew asleep except me on watch and the Sparky trying to raise someone on the long-wave radio, his failure adding to the feeling we were alone in the universe. Half asleep I set off down the deserted half-lit corridors towards the toilets. As I walked, I remembered a conversation with the engineers the day before. The ship's sewage all went down to a large tank into which enzymes were added. They munched the solids in the waste water until it was clean enough to discharge at sea. Now those little munching enzymes lived in a little universe of their own. Being born, eating, mating, fighting all-comers, and dying only to be eaten by the other enzymes. Given the random mutation of births and the survival of the fittest it was only a matter of time before a strain of enzyme evolved that was bigger and stronger than all the other enzymes. Slowly this muta- tion would get bigger and bigger, eating everything available, eventually evolving to a size where it could slime out of the tank and up through the complex of pipework towards daylight via a toilet bowl. As I said before, this image of some huge enzyme monster was slowly worming its way through my brain as I entered the toilet cubi- cle. The lid was down on the toilet. I slowly reached forward to raise it. Was the enzyme conga trapped under the lid, waiting to spring out? I decided to move to the next cubicle where the lid was already up, but sat down nervously.

4   Critique the following passage in terms of observation and explanation.

The Soldier

by

Rupert Brooke

If I should die, think only this of me:

That there's some corner of a foreign field

That is for ever England. There shall be

In that rich earth a richer dust concealed;

A dust whom England bore, shaped, made aware,

Gave, once, her flowers to love, her ways to roam,

A body of England's, breathing English air,

Washed by the rivers, blest by suns of home.

And think, this heart, all evil shed away,

A pulse in the eternal mind, no less

Gives somewhere back the thoughts by England given;

Her sights and sounds; dreams happy as her day;

And laughter, learnt of friends; and gentleness,

In hearts at peace, under an English heaven.

5   **Critique the following passage in terms of observation and explanation. Notice that the passage was used in the concerns chapter.**

There is a wonderful system of public footpaths throughout England. These give non-landowners the opportunity to romp through the countryside getting exercise, fresh air and a chance to admire England's wonderful scenery. Some of these pathways were established as legal public rights of way only after hard-fought political battles. Prior to the proclamation of a new footpath campaigners would often walk along the proposed routes to see what reaction they got from the landowners. There is a tale about one rather strong-willed walker bumping into an irate landowner. The quarrel went something like this:
   'Get off my land.'
   'What makes all this huge moorland only yours?'
   'It was given to my forefathers by the King of England.'
   'Why?' asked the walker.
   'For fighting alongside the king against the French at the Battle of Agincourt in 1415.'
   To which came the retort from the walker:
   'That sounds fair enough, mate. Take your jacket off and I'll fight you for it now.'

7 Using Metaphors to Critique

Critique the passage below by identifying the metaphors used. Is there any sort of theme to these metaphors, is there a pattern to them, have they any overall consistency?

The old British Empire can claim a couple of good points. One is that it made killing people, especially wives and slaves, a state monopoly. Another was that it spread the wonderful Scottish education system throughout the world. However, I fear that some ill-informed marketing managers have eyed up this well-designed product with an eye for profit, not the long-term welfare of their society. Much as has been done with Christmas, relationships, pop-corn and baseball hats. Perhaps fresh from selling doughnuts, educational marketers seem to have re-visualised knowledge as a product whereby the college professor has a product called knowledge which he or she gives to the customer, the student. Effective education becomes how can the product can be better packaged and more quickly passed over to the customer? The Scots knew that knowing, like exercising or dieting, requires the 'customer' to do all the work. It cannot be given, it has to be taken. The brain is a muscle not a bucket. Some education marketing managers have trouble with this, confusing the teaching materials with knowing. This is like confusing a bike with exercise.

A group of very serious scientists came up with a rather reductionist line of research. They wanted to know how the body stored memory. Where was it, how was it turned into chemicals? One stream of this research involved training some worms to straighten, rather than curl up, when zapped with a small electrical current. Having passed their final test the worms were then thrown into a food mixer and reduced to a milkshake. This foodstuff was then fed to other 'unconditioned' worms, who then started doing the conditioned response of straightening rather than curling up, when electrocuted. What does this prove? Maybe that memory is a protein. Now if we could just train numerous worms each with a different bit of knowledge we could offer an education where people choose from a selection of worms, colour coded maybe. Perhaps education could be strange-tasting milkshake.

Try and avoid any distinction between metaphors, similes, analogies or tropes in general. Merely focus on the use of words to form distinct mental images in your head. The words that do this for me are centred on the words 'knowledge' and 'brain'. Knowledge is (not) like a product, or a protein; knowing is like fitness; knowledge cannot be poured. The brain is like a muscle; the brain is not like a bucket. My take on the passage is that the author is attempting to encourage the reader to resist the image (root metaphor) of knowledge as a 'thing' that can be given, like worm-flavoured milk shake. An alternative image (root metaphor) is provided of knowledge as a 'thing that has to be taken', like exercise or dieting. Giving is turned to taking.

Another take on the overall image (root metaphor) generated by the passage may be one of 'chastising'. The author is telling educators off for misunderstanding the nature of knowledge. Alternatively, the root metaphor of 'acquisition' might also be identified.

Before discussing metaphors in more general terms, a little more learning by induction may be useful. In the next passage what image is driving the author's writing?

Historians would call it technology. I try and avoid calling it science. The people that actually do it call themselves engineers. Engineers have freed us from the tyranny of nature and the hardships of a Third World life style. In my opinion there has been an excessive backlash against technology, especially energy technology from the warm and fat. Of course, we must demand the highest possible environmental standards but we and developing nations need protection from the cruelty of nature. Our grandparents have been witnesses to an incredible reduction of back-breaking, time-consuming tasks, both in industry and in the home. Elderly people often say that the greatest thing to happen in their lives was the introduction of cars and electricity. It allowed massive changes in education, justice and democracy. The exploitative class system was undermined by modern transport, communications, books and TV. Whatever environmental damage dams, power stations, transport and energy infrastructure have done is regretful but necessary. A farmer with a scythe would nearly work himself to death just gathering enough food for his own family. With a tractor he can feed a small town. We should be very proud of our engineers; they have saved us from endless misery and labour.

The individual images I identify after reading this passage are those of 'the tyranny of work', nature as tyranny, life as misery, life as hard work, and technology as a saviour. Therefore, my feeling is that the root metaphor or image in the author's head that is driving him or her to write is one of 'poverty' or 'starvation'. Alternatively it is one of 'liberating technology'.

History

The study of metaphors was the providence of literature, not science, until recent times. Poetry and metaphor were the flowers, the emotive language of the arts. Scientists writing up their experiments were told not to use metaphors, to stick to a direct explanation of the facts. Marshall McLuhan, in his critique of the media (newspapers, television, etc.), made popular the idea that most if not all words were metaphors. Things are described in terms of other things: words or sounds. If you are asked to name a new street or hybrid fruit you will use existing words even if you mix two together. Else you may try and turn a sound into a word, such as 'scrunch'. Even numbers can be seen to alter the mental image of what is being spoken: the mental image of one bird is different to ten birds. The ease of identification of words as metaphors diminishes with use. At one time a company was metaphorically described as like a biological organism, an organisation. We now directly equate the word 'organisation' with companies. Now we need fresher metaphors for an organisation such as a 'mental prison', 'a brain' or 'orchestrated greed'.

Characteristics

Ortney (1975) in his paper entitled 'Why metaphors are necessary and not just nice' argues that metaphors have three characteristics: compactness, vividness and inexpressibility. Compactness refers to the ability of metaphors to communicate an analogous mental image, saving longer explanations. Vividness provides motivation or impact, while inexpressibility deals with overcoming problems of the limitation of vocabulary. Moreover Richards (1936) identifies metaphors as being usefully identified in terms of the topic, the vehicle, the ground and the tension. So in the metaphor, he is as strong as a lion, the topic is strength, the vehicle is a lion, the ground is the commonality between the man's strength and a lion, while the tension is what is not intended by the metaphor. Metaphors are, and sometimes need a lot of, interpretation.

Root metaphors

Metaphors appear to exist at least at two levels: one is in the simple form of 'he is as strong as a lion' and the other is as a viewpoint driving an entire passage. This second, less explicit form has been highlighted by writers like Pepper (1942) and Lahoff (1993) who point out that all passages are written from a particular perspective, or root metaphor, which can usually be picked up from consideration of some of the specific words used in the passage. This is often a hidden persuader in the passage. For example, it is possible to show that science is based on the root metaphor of 'seeing'. Scientific papers use words like observation: 'see what is meant' and 'the conclusion is seen to be proven'. Another example is that computers are often described in terms of three-dimensional space:

'storage space', capacity, 'inside the computer' and 'input'. Social scientists often use a root metaphor of 'subjects' in their research. This carries connotations of hierarchy with subjects being less aware of their own behaviours than the researchers.

There was a flood of papers that appeared in the 1980s and early 1990s trying to identify root metaphors in various human activities. These seem to have been motivated by Morgan's classic book, *Images of Organisations* (1986). In this he classified the literature on organisational theory by root metaphor. For example, the most common root or implicit metaphor used in the early twentieth century to write about organisations was 'machine'. Employees were described as cogs in that machine, organisations were finely tuned machines. This root metaphor led to management practices that included work study, employees' every move was carefully analysed for inefficient actions, and new employees were measured for their ability to carry loads up and down stairs. Another of Morgan's root metaphors was 'adaptive organism', which encourages a more market competitive view of the activities of organisations. Others include 'information processing brain', psychic prison and self-reproducing system.

As an example of how vivid words might be synthesised into a root metaphor I recently asked some fellow academics for metaphors to describe a summary of the previous research articles often provided at the start of a research thesis: the literature review. Their suggestions are listed below. I have separated them into two as I felt there were two root metaphors.

Group 1: These said a review of the literature was like:

- **a map ('go where you like')**

- **a detective (seeking clues for new research directions)**

- **a beachcomber (sifting through others' castoffs)**

- **a prospector (seeking gems or nuggets)**

- **a lens (to focus readers)**

- **pathfinder (lay out an area and point to key sources)**

- **sifting and winnowing**

- **a funnel (funnelling in)**

- **a signpost (to find your empirics)**

- **a concertina (narrowing and enlarging your search, like a concertina windbag)**

- **a focus mechanism (you are talking about this, not that)**

- **releasing the imagination**

The root metaphor I allocated to this group was 'investigation' (seeking out, discovery, detection, journey). Under this image of a literature review, preparing one is like a search for (in) the unknown, going out to find out something you don't know.

Group 2: These thought a literature review was like:

- **expert witnesses in court**

- **currency (to buy credibility)**

- **building blocks**

- **a concrete foundation**

- **the history**

- **a mirror (to see oneself in context)**

- **a requirements document**

- **a credibility filter (whose work do you draw on; what is the source of your ideas?)**

- **due diligence (have you acknowledged others whose ideas you draw on?)**

- **social courtesy (can you be relied on not to steal ideas?)**

- **a situational context (what conversation is this paper a part of?)**

- **a family tree**

- **a foundation (you are educated and building on a tradition)**

- **a puzzle (your idea fits into this larger puzzle)**

These metaphors of a literature review I thought might be allocated the root metaphor of 'court' or 'prosecution' (justification, evidence, proof, argument). The literature is used to support a reasoned argument, justify a conjecture, or validate a hunch.

It is hard to provide exact direction on how to spot root metaphors. All I can suggest is that you read through the passage and write down any words that seem vivid, emotive or even laboured to you. These may be verbs, adjectives or nouns. From this list ask yourself if there is a collective name, theme or root metaphor that could be used to sum up the list.

Attempt to identify a root metaphor in the passage below.

I had flown down to board a ship as it came into a port in the South Island of New Zealand. Hardly aboard, the radio officer asked me in for a drink. He was Welsh, large, jovial and was celebrating the news that he was being flown home for some leave after ten years doing a run I would soon become familiar with. The ship ran dairy foods from New Zealand to the West Indies, and returned with a cargo of rum. The life of a radio officer was a lonely one: four hours on duty, four hours off, round the clock when at sea, sitting alone in the radio room. We had a heavy night, and early the next morning I gingerly inspected the hold space before cargo loading got started. The inspection finished, I watched the loading through the morning. It was uneventful except for the figure of Sparkie staggering off down to the pub at about 10 a.m. I thought it strange he was in full uniform, but assumed he was celebrating in style. It was early afternoon before he staggered back. As he went to walk up the gangplank he slipped and fell into the dock water between the ship and the wharf. At first, we thought it was funny, he was in little danger from being squashed as the ship was tied to a post on the side of a pier. If anything his greatest risk seemed to be from the rubbish floating on the water. A few of us ran over to help him up, but it soon became clear that we could not reach him; he was too far down. We became concerned when we saw he was floating motionless face down. Ten minutes later someone got to him in a small boat but he was dead; apparently drunken people often inhale on impact with water. The ship had to sail before the funeral so we were at sea when we got a radio call from the cemetery priest saying there was no one attending Sparkie's funeral. He wondered what he should do. One of the more enlightened ship's crew asked the priest to postpone the funeral until the next day. Meanwhile, he radio-phoned a brothel and agreed to pay six women to get dressed up in their best working clothes and to attend the funeral service. The priest rang back to say the funeral was a unique one.

It is a personal interpretation but I would identify the root metaphor as 'loneliness'. The remote location of the incident, a life at sea, the lone efforts of a radio officer on duty, the end of a ten-year tour, the coming back from the pub alone, and the absence of friends or family can all be synthesised into a lonely life and death, dictated by a career choice.

Summary

This chapter has suggested a critique stance that identifies the root metaphor in a passage. This is the overall image that the passage communicates, a collective or meta metaphor. Exactly how you identify this root metaphor is hard to explain. One possibility is to identify all the distinctive words used in the passage and see if they suggest some overall concept. It is a rather intuitive exercise but when done well can provide great insight to a passage.

Metaphor questions

The above discussion has been summarised into a series of questions you might ask yourself about a passage in order to critique it using the root metaphor stance:

- **What are the vivid verbs, adjectives or nouns used?**

- **What are the novel verbs, adjectives or nouns used?**

- **What are the emotional verbs, adjectives or nouns used?**

- **What is the mood set by the passage?**

- **What is the topic under consideration in the passage? How is this described?**

- **Can you identify any explicit metaphors in the passage? Can these be generalised to the entire passage?**

- **To which of your senses does the passage appeal?**

Exercises

1 **Critique the following passage by identifying a root metaphor.**

I heard this story from Frank, who was an animal behaviourist at Adelaide University and a great supporter of the local zoo. It was about the uncanny ability of the big cats to spot weakness in potential prey. I assume this skill has been evolved from the need to select one particular animal to focus their attack upon when stalking a herd. The meat of an antelope which has a slight limp tastes much the same as the meat of a perfectly fit one, but it is easier to catch. Apparently, if a visitor to the zoo limps past the front of a big cat's cage, it is possible to observe the big cat suddenly sit up and show a keen interest.

2   **Critique the following passage by identifying a root metaphor.**

Talking of cats, there are special problems with owning a much loved moggy when you live in Australia, given its large snake population. What do you do when your darling pet comes staggering home with the familiar two pinprick marks in its body? It happened to a family man I knew. Naturally, the kids screamed with panic and howled for the vet. Dad was more pragmatic, trying to point out that they had other cats, that the antidote would most likely be expensive and often did not work, that the cat was old, that cats killed small native animals and that you could get a free kitten anywhere. When they all got to the vet, they were asked if it was a Brown Snake, Tiger Snake, Red-bellied Snake or what. They did not know. The vet explained that some anti-venom was cheaper than others, but if they did not know the exact snake type he would have to give the whole range, which would be expensive. Dad suddenly remembered it was a Brown Snake, but the youngest of the family pointed out he was only saying that because that was the cheapest option. So Dad winced and agreed to the full programme, the injections were given, and the cat died.

3   **Critique the following passage by identifying a root metaphor. Notice that the passage was also used in the observation chapter.**

Many years ago and after many hours of rolling cannon balls down inclined planes, Galileo got into a dispute with his fellow lecturers. They were lecturing to their students that if two weights were dropped from a height the heaviest would hit the ground first. Galileo disagreed, so they decided to conduct an experiment to decide the matter. They went to the top of the Leaning Tower of Pisa and started dropping cannon balls over the top balcony in twos, one large and one small. Unfortunately an argument started about exactly how to line up the two balls at their starting position and how to be sure both were released at exactly the same time. The landing was also hard to measure. Some preliminary trials soon revealed you need some very accurate measuring devices to be able to detect which ball actually did hit the ground first. Moreover, the lighter ball appeared to move faster to start with but then heavy one tended to catch up. Observation was (as ever) proving to raise more questions than it solved. Galileo then came up with a thought experiment. He reasoned that if a large cannon ball and a small one were melted together into a larger cannon ball then his ball would have the average speed of the original balls. Now if you dropped all three, the new largest ball cannot fall the fastest because it is the average speed of the other two; however, it is the largest ball so should fall the fastest. This dilemma is only solved if all three balls hit the ground together.

Using Contradictions to Critique

Critique the following passage in terms of identifying any tensions that are not explicitly addressed but that are driving the situation presented.

Why are Santa Claus's clothes the same red and white as Coca-Cola's corporate colours? There are many shades of red, so why are they identical? The Americans have commercialised a lot of European traditions into popular lookalike products, such as baseball hats and doughnuts. With Santa they took Saint Nicholas and gave him a marketing makeover. When I was a child I vaguely remember a maroon and green, as well as a red and white, Father Christmas. Nowadays they are all Coca-Cola red and white. When in Texas recently, I noticed the cans of Coke had Santa's ghost-like head merged into the design. Is Santa just a Coca-Cola advert? I must admit I have no mental image of him handing out Coke, but maybe that would offend too many people. I assume the basis of the tradition of a Coca-Cola-coloured Santa, like flying reindeer and the song 'I'm dreaming of a white Christmas', are merely a Christmas image created by Hollywood moviemakers in the 1930s. Is our culture really so thin? Lemmings do not suicide off cliffs unless thrown by moviemakers, tigers don't live in Africa and Egyptians did not have slaves to build the pyramids. Moreover, the Christian Church resisted the celebration of Christmas for the first four centuries, because it was thought it would be confused with a well-established pagan midwinter ritual in northern Europe that used images of red berries, white snow, green mistletoe leaves and talked of the rebirth of the earth after the shortest day.

My critique of this passage would start with the three most obvious artefacts in the passage: Coke, Santa and Christmas. The underlying contradictions in Coke suggested by the passage are the complex interaction between a marketing strategy and a traditional ritual. I assume Coke wants to have red and white images presented before us as often as possible. If Santa is wearing Coke's corporate colours then every well-intentioned community activity to evoke the historic ritual of Santa becomes a Coke advert. The tension is between Coke's right to advertise and our right to unendorsed ritual.

The image of Santa is itself an icon that generates huge tensions between generous well-meaning gift giving and massive social and market pressures to overspend. This often leads to antisocial behaviour like increased levels of family violence. Christmas is a further contradiction between the use of the visuals and trappings that suggest a north European midwinter ritual of snow, evergreen trees and hot foods, and images that celebrate of the birth of Jesus in semi-desert conditions.

Seeking contradictions

Identifying inherent contradictions, paradoxes, underlying tensions or forces is like 'looking behind' or 'looking underneath' the passage. Karl Marx used the now famous example of observing a caterpillar. No matter how carefully you measure and count details about the caterpillar, unless you know about the butterfly, and the laws of evolution, you do not really understand the caterpillar. Sowell (1985) argues contradiction was Marx's own research methodology where he saw inherited privilege and the control of what we today would call 'knowledge' (the means of production) as the underlying forces that created the dreadfully oppressive class systems in Britain in the mid nineteenth century.[4] We take this for granted now. He felt that this political and economic system had to be changed if the outcome, poverty, was to be combated. Improvements in education and health for the masses in the twentieth century began a process of changing the knowledge base, paid for by death taxes, which has eased the situation in the developed nations. Engels, who worked closely with Marx, saw analogies between the tensions in society and the tensions in nature.[5] The underlying tension in nature is a physical competition for survival. If one species is to survive then it has to kill another, just as happens when you eat a burger. However, as is seen in the evolution of species in nature, these dialectic forces can be creative.

With the contradicting stance of critique, what is seen as an artefact or a phenomenon is understood to be the result of hidden forces in tension. For example, the design of a building, a vehicle, or any system is the result of various technical, organisational and personal tensions. The same is true of Christmas celebrations, which can be seen to be the outcome resulting from the underlying tensions of pagan ritual, the desire for midwinter celebrations, Christian Church concerns over maintaining power and influence, and economics. Contradictions between those with wealth and those without cause the creation of a police force; contradictions between ideologies cause wars.

Types

It is tempting to identify types of contradictions. The one we have identified so far is the contradictions that cause a particular artefact to exist in a certain form. Another is the result of the presence of the artefact. So, with an artefact like a mobile phone, it causes contradictions between our desire to communicate with those we cannot see, various technologies, commercial interests and self-image issues, which have struggled to result in the outcome that is the present mobile phone phenomenon. However, the phone itself provides contradictions such as both giving and taking away personal freedom, and extending while thinning down social relationships. They are at least two 'faced' (Janus faced), perhaps three or more.

Nielsen (1996) and Mason (1969; 1996) identified various types of contradictions that might be useful to understand social systems like commercial organisations. Nielsen defines contradiction in terms of dialectic, 'change that emerges from the interplay of conflict and among differences and affirmation of areas of agreement'. He argues (in a dialectic with the reader?) that these change processes differ in terms of emotionality, they do not have to be quarrelsome, aggressive or conflictive, but they can be. Identifying these types of dialectic contradictions can form a further stance of critiquing articles.

His first 'ideas' contradiction involves asking yourself who is arguing with whom over what idea in the passage? Is the argument intended to enable one side to win or to encourage the development of improved ideas? In the Santa passage there was a hint of a suggestion that product developers were playing with traditional artefacts as ideas to make them available as viable, if impoverished, commercial products. It is hard to imagine the early Church wanting to think creatively with the followers of pagan practices about improved rituals.

Nielsen's second contradiction he calls 'action', drawing on the 'act, reflect, act' learning loops of Argyris and Schon (1996). The contradiction is between what is said and what is done. The classic example here is an organisation plan (words) that says something is important but the budget (the action) allocates very little to that activity. In the passage above a contradiction, a tension of this type could be identified between the Christian meaning of Christmas as a birth and the use of Christmas trees and midwinter images.

Nielsen's third contradiction is that of 'voice' where one human group develops their understandings and actions without wanting to be informed by others. In the passage above the product developers want to make cheap commercial 'lookalikes' of traditional artefacts for profit, without asking the traditional owners/users of that artefact what they think or feel. One reason may be that the developers do not want to have to deal with the 'complaints' of the traditional users who may be a whole community. Second, there can be a feeling that the traditional community will not understand or have different priorities. As a result of 'fear of confrontation', knowledge is lost.

The last of Nielsen's contradictions that will be identified here is caused by a vying for 'resources'. Human action can easily be seen as an endless process of vying for resources with other people and species. This can used to critique the Santa passage by commenting upon the pressure on people to make a living. In this struggle to make resources and profits flow in their direction, rather than to others, people invent popular products. The early Church could be seen as vying for the resource of people's souls, or more cynically for people's expenditure, when offering forgiveness for sins.

Critique the following passage by identifying the contradictions that created any artefacts, and then the contradictions caused by these artefacts.

> Some friends of mine once came home from holiday to find their large patio (ranch-style) glass sliding doors smashed. Nothing was taken from the house, which left my friends a bit confused. They got the doors replaced for some huge cost. However, when they returned home from work a few days later they found the doors again broken. They replaced them, complaining to the builder that there must be something wrong with the glass or the frame. Was it self-destructing, or perhaps it was something to do with temperature changes through the day? The builder pointed out that it required a sledgehammer to break the glass. Shortly after the second new door had been installed, one family member noticed that the neighbour's Billy Goat had got into their garden. When she went to chase it away, it headed for her house. When the goat got to the patio it suddenly reacted to a reflection of itself in the door windows. It lowered its head and started forward to head-butt this 'rival' ram.

What you identify as the underlying tensions in this passage is a personal choice. It makes me reflect on the inherent contradiction of glass. It blocks most of the senses, apart from seeing. It blocks the cold to some extent, noise to some extent, smell well, but allows us to see through it, lets light through it. The tension is that in order to have these attributes it is brittle. There is another tension of having animals like a ram near something brittle, which is not common in nature. From the ram's perspective the tension is apparent: the rival male goat needs to be encouraged to move on.

The 'idea' dialectic may stimulate thoughts that the passage is providing a novel idea about how the glass doors became broken, but in the sense of legal argument the evidence is weak. The people in the passage have debated the problem with the builder but not in a comprehensive manner, so the idea contradiction has not been used to be creative. Seeing the goat attempt to butt the glass only really provides an idea worthy of further investigation. Perhaps the solutions may be to use contradiction to create innovative ideas.

Thinking about the 'action' dialectic may stimulate thoughts about the house owners only having a little engineering experience and not appreciating the sort of force required to smash the glass compared with the forces involved in temperature changes in glass. Perhaps if they had experienced trying to break or bend the glass they may have focused earlier on livestock being involved.

The 'voice' dialectic raises questions in my mind about who was excluded from the discussions. It is assumed that the most experienced voice in terms of windows would be the builder, in terms of 'break and entry' it would be the police, and the most experienced in terms of local issues would be the owners. The missing voice was that of the ram. Getting that would be hard, but appreciating the problem from the animal's perspective may not be too hard.

The 'vying for resources' dialectic seems to be mainly between the house owners and the vendors of a brittle glass door. If it is too brittle for the task of being a door, then the house owners will want their money back. I cannot help but also identify the goat's grab for resources. It wants to take over the territory of its neighbour, even if that involves butting out a mythical challenging ram who lives in the house.

Summary

A critique stance that has an impressive track record for encouraging social change is that of trying to identify the paradoxes, the contradictions or the underlying tensions in a passage. Opposing tensions often act to design particular outcomes, such as democratic processes or resource negotiation routines. The presence of artefacts also creates tensions. For example, the Internet provides the freedom to search for information, and the responsibility to do so.

Contradiction questions

The above discussion can be summarised into the following series of questions which you might ask yourself about any passage in order to critique it using the seeking contradictions stance.

General

- Why are any artefacts mentioned in the passage 'two faced'?

- What underlying tensions designed the artefacts in the passage?

Ideas

- Does the passage set up any sort of dialectic between two alternatives?

- Can you think of any alternatives that might (also) be included to encourage more thought about the contents of the passage?

- Is the author suitably suspicious of his or her own conclusion?

- Are improvements to the ideas under suspicion being suggested?

Action

- Is there any evidence of actions and words not being aligned?

- Was there any action undertaken simply as a 'let's try it and see what happens?'

- Was there any sort of reflection or post-mortem involved in the passage? Was it effective?

- Was there any response to unanticipated actions? If so, did it lead to learning?

Voice

- Is the passage blocking the voice of 'others' in any way?

- Was everybody involved in the contents of the passage given a chance to explain from their point of view?

- Was there any consideration of how 'radicals' or 'a devil's advocate' would have responded to the activities depicted?

Resources

- Can you identify any underlying tensions between human groups vying for resources?

Exercises

1   **Use the idea of seeking inherent contradictions to critique the following passage. These may be contradictions that created an artefact or that result from the presence of the artefact.**

I am perfectly at ease with the selfish gene argument that the main purpose of life is children, and in providing for those children. It is the genes that are important, not the person. However, as a modern dad I am amused to notice how the role of children has changed in one, my, generation. As a teenager I, proverbially, was a 'strapper' (as in saddling up a horse) for my father but now I am the 'strapper' for my daughters. Increased wealth and excess of food has changed children from an extra pair of hands to help mum and dad into an expensive toy. I am of an age to remember tales of my grandfather coming home to an evening meal after a day's hard physical work. He was the only family member to have meat in his evening meal; the kids had the dripping (fat). There was not enough money for everyone to have meat and he needed all his strength to work. Modern farming methods, including chemicals, have reversed that situation in one generation so that, if anything, my children (and me) have to discipline themselves not to eat too much red meat. The increased wealth that follows this food surplus now means dad has a well-paid soft job and has time for hobbies, exercise, extensive volunteer activities and time to play with the kids, all of which were nearly impossible for my grandfather. At the turn of the century the insurance companies in the Western world acknowledged the changing economics of children in families by not allowing parents to insure for the loss of their children. Previously, and still for farmers in the Third World, children were an asset because they are cheap labour. As the wealth of a country increases, and it urbanises, the children turn from an asset to a liability. In modern times the death of a child reduces the financial burden on the parent. Therefore in the West you cannot insure for the loss of your child; you cannot insure against a reduction in costs.

2   **Use the idea of seeking inherent contradictions to critique the following passage. These may be contradictions that created an artefact or that result from the presence of the artefact.**

As a teenager I was trained as a navigator in the merchant navy – a great profession, with a great history. I've been back and forth across the Pacific using the sun, stars like Betelgeuse, a couple of very good clocks, practice and six-figure log tables to plot a position on a chart. However, the profession of navigator has now largely gone the way of many old professions, a victim of technology. Now, you read a dial from a GPS satellite message. But all that expertise was not wasted. I am here to tell you that whenever you visit a strange town and cannot see the sun, you should know where the main TV transmitter is located. All the homeowners' TV aerials point to the transmitter. If you get lost, just look at the aerials on top of houses, and it is as good as looking at a compass.

3   Use the idea of seeking inherent contradictions to critique the following passage. These may be contradictions that created an artefact or that result from the presence of the artefact. Notice that this passage was used in Chapter 7.

The old British Empire can claim a couple of good points. One is that it made killing people, especially wives and slaves, a state monopoly. Another was that it spread the wonderful Scottish education system throughout the world. However, I fear that some ill-informed marketing managers have eyed up this well-designed product with an eye for profit, not the long-term welfare of their society. Much as has been done with Christmas, relationships, pop-corn and baseball hats. Perhaps fresh from selling doughnuts, educational marketers seem to have re-visualised knowledge as a product whereby the college professor has a product called knowledge which he or she gives to the customer, the student. Effective education becomes how can the product be better packaged and more quickly passed over to the customer? The Scots knew that knowing, like exercising or dieting, requires the 'customer' to do all the work. It cannot be given, it has to be taken. The brain is a muscle not a bucket. Some education marketing managers have trouble with this, confusing the teaching materials with knowing. This is like confusing a bike with exercise.

A group of very serious scientists came up with a rather reductionist line of research. They wanted to know how the body stored memory. Where was it, how was it turned into chemicals? One stream of this research involved training some worms to straighten, rather than curl up, when zapped with a small electrical current. Having passed their final test the worms were then thrown into a food mixer and reduced to a milkshake. This foodstuff was then fed to other 'unconditioned' worms, who then started doing the conditioned response of straightening rather than curling up, when electrocuted. What does this prove? Maybe that memory is a protein. Now if we could just train numerous worms each with a different bit of knowledge we could offer an education where people choose from a selection of worms, colour coded maybe. Perhaps education could be strange-tasting milkshake.

9 Using an Evolutionary Stance to Critique

Critique the following as if the entire passage is a new mutation of a virus. Ask yourself:

- **What were the laws of evolution that evolved this virus (passage) from the millions of paragraphs written in the past?**

- **Why did this particular passage end up here at the top of this chapter?**

- **What did its parents look like?**

> I like to think I have heard the lot when it comes to students making excuses about exam performance. He started by explaining that he had just started with a new girlfriend. Reason enough to do badly, but his real problem was his girlfriend's ex-boyfriend who was not taking her decision as well as he might. Rather, he had pursued the new couple relentlessly with a large knife talking about castration, while boasting of his previous criminal record. The student summed all this up by pointing out that the stalker was a meatworker from the local abattoir. But the student really won me over by pointing out that he did not want special consideration for his exams, it was just the meatworker knew he would have to attend the exams. The student was also concerned for me if the meatworker burst into the exam-room wielding a knife. He wanted to reassure me he would think none the worse of me if I merely pointed him out; he was perfectly willing to orchestrate his own exit. What he wanted from me was some consideration from my marking, if he had to run.

My thoughts are that the original virus was born in the niche environment of a university staff tearoom. The passage seems to have survived in an environment of concern for how to distinguish genuine study problems from rorts (scams). It would have been repeated because it was a little humorous and involves a little danger. It was plausible, and about the right length to be told over a tea break. It would have died in the environment of an official 'appeals court' report owing to its lack of specific detail or as material for a night-club comic routine as it is 'grey', not explicit humour. It has mutated itself into a written passage because the author, by writing the book, created a new environment in which it was well suited. The written mutation has becomes asynchronous, independent of the life or location of the author. The popularity of its new host, this book, will determine its reproduction rate, its survival. Moreover, it is capable of reproducing back into an oral story but unlikely ever to be replicated in other written stories.

Evolution stance

The evolution (or meme) stance draws on the metaphor of an article being like a virus, a biological entity which survives and reproduces depending on the environment it finds itself operating within. For more on evolution theory read Darwin, Dawkins (1989) and Dennett (1996). It is not necessary to get into a debate about the evolution of humans to use the stance. Things either evolve or they stay exactly the same over time. Planets, continents, species, organisations, people and ideas evolve. Evolution theory tends to focus at the species level, but it has also been used to explain the design of living things, the structure of the neural connections in your brain and the development of your immune system. Words evolve; pathetic no longer means tearful and bureaucratic no longer means through rational rules. Ideas evolve; policy formulation used to be under-taken by collecting the best brains together, but now it involves collecting together those who are involved or concerned. Intelligence was once thought to be a genetic attribute, but now it is a mix of nature and nurture, perhaps reflecting intrinsic long-term motiva-tion rather than processing capacity.

The basic tenets of evolution include the following.

Sexually reproduced offspring are a random genetic variation on the genetic possibilities of the parents. Asexual reproduction, as practised by some very small life forms, means the young have identical genetic structure to their 'mother'. Sexual reproduction mixes up the genetic structure of the mother and father, causing a wider range of genetic diver-sity. Species that do this seem to have survived, including humans. Without this diversity plagues like the Black Death may have killed all humans, not just a large percentage. This can be used as a stance for critique by asking what mixed together to produce the passage under consideration? What were its parents like? They may well have contrasting attrib-utes in the way two explosive gases, oxygen and hydrogen, make up life-sustaining water. Alternative parents for the meatworker passage might be seen as love and murder. The parents may also be seen as being the major influences on the author, the genus being the school of thought the article comes from. The degree of variation is how different the article is from the parents, who may or may not admire their offspring's features, but the environment will decide success, whether later authors are influenced by (cite) it.

More are born than will reproduce. The attributes of the offspring determine if they survive long enough to reproduce in their environment. The environment at the time the offspring are growing to reproductive maturity determines whether they are able to reproduce their particular attributes to another generation. Millions of seeds, sperm, eggs are produced but only a very few make it through to reproduce. The rest are victims to their environment including competition from their own kind. See *Sperm Wars* (Baker, 2000). Something like a Gum or Pepper Tree produces millions of seeds every year of which only a very few will ever result in a seed-giving tree.

The appropriate level of analysis for life becomes the gene pool or the survival of the species, not the individual. A butterfly may only live for a matter of days; it does not eat and seems merely to be a mechanism to move caterpillars from bush to bush. The butterfly's life only makes sense if you think in terms of the life of the genes, not the container or body they presently reside in. The genes of a species live for millions of years, constantly renewing and redesigning their container with each birth and death. Birth and death are seen as essential to improving adaptability to the environment. Species are designed by this process.

This can be used as a stance to critique by thinking about all those passages that did not survive. Why did this one survive; was it totally random or were there particular forces involved; could more have survived? Passages about love and murder flourish everywhere; they are a very successful species. Stories of love without mention of some sort of adversity are not so interesting and tend to die out, perhaps because there is no tension. Survival as a passage might require it to have some internal tension. The passage can also be thought of as an offspring, a virus mutation, something born of the author's life.

Here is another example. Critique this by asking how it has evolved, from what and how?

> After reading about David Hume's chapter on cause and effect and pondering his comments that we cannot anticipate an 'effect' just from the attributes of something we call a 'cause', I went to have a wash. To my delight my young daughter saw me and ran to join me in the washroom. She climbed up on the small chair we had placed to one side of the washbasin so as to help me have my wash. As I went to turn on the taps she said, 'Do you want hot water?' 'Yes please,' I replied. Her chair was right next to the hot water tap side of the basin. She turned on the tap nearest to her and felt the water. 'It is cold,' she said with a little sigh, 'But don't worry, I can make it hot.' 'How?' I said. 'You have to hold your finger under the running water and that makes it go hot!'

There are millions of pages of philosophy that have been written about the validity of 'cause and effect' knowledge claims; a light switch seems to 'cause' the 'effect' of a light going on. There have also been millions of proud parents talking about the amusing interpretations of their young children. This passage represents a mating of these two species to produce another which has so far survived in an environment of university students who are aware of the problem around issues of cause and effect (research, regression and decision making). There is a whole species of lecturer–parent stories where proud parents see analogies between their children's activities and some theoretical concept they wish to communicate to students. There is a particular herding around children's books. One subspecies is the use of the 'Cat in the Hat' series to teach system thinking concepts.

For academic articles the evolution critique stance can use the academic journal publication industry as the environment. So publication of an article may be analogous to birth; working papers and drafts can be seen as failures to reach birth, and the environment the audience. Some species can alter their environment in order to survive, others cannot. So, when critiquing an academic article, if possible examine the references and sources as the parents.

Evolution questions

Ask yourself the following questions about the article:

- **Can you identify earlier mutations of the passage virus?**

- **Is there any sign of a merging of two or more viruses to breed this passage virus?**

- **What are the attributes of the passage virus that have helped it survive?**

- **What environment might have treated the passage virus differently?**

- **What will determine the success of the passage virus in the future to multiply and dominate its environment?**

Exercises

1   **Critique the following passage using the evolution stance.**

People claim that they dreamt about a train or plane crash before it happened and saved someone's life by convincing them not to travel. I am sure they are right, but it does not mean the dreamer has any special gift, apart from being a caring

continued

continued

human being. The most obvious question these claims raise is how many times has that person wrongfully dreamt of crashes and how many other people also wrongly dream of crashes every night? But more importantly, such claims miss the point of dreams. Dreams are a good indicator of your anxieties. Falling, being chased, and losing loved ones, all cause pretty standard dreams. For example, dreaming you are back at school years after you left, just prior to an interview or test, is fairly common.

With dreams that involve fear of dying, like crashes or falls, I suggest you force the dream to come to its violent conclusion because your brain obviously has no experience of death.

We do not see using only our eyes. The largest part of what you see comes from anticipation of the brain. The brain is like a room full of shouting people and the eyes are only one voice. The senses, including memory and logic, are the others. Given a lack of concentration and the memory's apparently very loud voice it is possible for the brain to 'see' things the eyes have not observed. Visions of dead loved ones are an obvious example. A bad dream is simply your anxieties shouting very loudly when your eyes are resting.

2   **Critique the following passage using the evolution stance. Notice that the passage was used in the contradictions chapter.**

Some friends of mine once came home from holiday to find their large patio (ranch-style) glass sliding doors smashed. Nothing was taken from the house, which left my friends a bit confused. They got the door replaced for some huge cost. However, when they returned home from work a few days later they found the doors again broken. They replaced them, complaining to the builder that there must be something wrong with the glass or the frame. Was it self-destructing, or perhaps it was something to do with temperature changes through the day? The builder pointed out that it required a sledgehammer to break the glass. Shortly after the second new door had been installed, one family member noticed that the neighbour's Billy Goat had got into their garden. When she went to chase it away, it headed for her house. When the goat got to the patio it suddenly reacted to a reflection of itself in the door windows. It lowered its head and started forward to head-butt this 'rival' ram.

10 Using Irony, Paradox and Humour to Critique

Can you identify from the following passage two things that seem to be true but that contradict each other, a paradox? For example, it seems a paradox that dogs are not as intelligent as humans but it is humans that go out to work every day to feed dogs.

> Owing to some excessive inbreeding between the early Dutch immigrants to South Africa there were a number of whites in the South Africa of the 1970s who would not have won an IQ contest. But as they were white, under apartheid, they had to be secured jobs which provided them with more status than blacks. I experienced one of these whites driving a dockside crane used to load general cargo onto ships. As an apprentice on the ship it was one of my jobs to ensure the ship's freshwater tanks were filled using the valves on the dockside. I noticed the leg of a crane was positioned over the water valve so tried to shout up to the white driver asking him to move the crane a fraction. Apart from language difficulties it soon became obvious that the driver was confused by what I was asking. Eventually a supervisor came along and asked what was going on. I explained. He responded by climbing up into the crane-driver's cab and assisted the driver to move the crane. When I had finished with the water valve I started to shout up to the crane-driver to say he could now move back if he wished. The supervisor again noticed, walked over to me slowly, put his hand on my shoulder and said, 'No son, not twice in one day.'

The paradox that strikes me is that it is true under apartheid law that whites are superior to blacks, while it is true under nature that there are going to be whites who are not as intelligent as blacks. When these two realities meet, problems are going to occur.

Defining irony, paradox and humour

Using paradox and its sisters, irony and humour, as a critique 'tool' has a huge history in the arts, in literature and painting. However, in social science it is seen more as a problem than as an insight to alternative stances on the world (Lewis, 2000; Rorty, 1989). Consider a very well-known quote:

> We shape our buildings; thereafter they shape us. (Winston Churchill)

It is both true that we design our buildings and that they design our lives. The design of buildings can have a significant effect on our lives, an obvious example being their size, their cost, the provision of heating or cooling, and the availability of dry and sufficient light, as well as the provision of common meeting places. A building designed to allow social interaction may encourage more creativity. The first part of Churchill's statement is the traditional stance of science that we are in control of nature and designing buildings to our specifications. The second part, however, starts to open up a stance where we, as both the users and designers of buildings, are the product of our environment. The second stance also opens up thoughts of a feedback loop in the relationship between our buildings and us. Churchill encourages us to see two stances in relationship with each other. This may stimulate thought, a good basis for critique.

That irony, paradox and humour can encourage thought suggests that they work by creating some sort of cognitive dissonance, and/or logical jumps, between stances. Reminiscent of cognitive switching, the differing stances are not expected to provide explanations about the gaps between themselves. The dissonance is thought to be decentring and encouraging the brain to go into a state of rapid sense making, or at least be open to the senses while attempting to interpret inconsistencies.

The arts have not missed this opportunity to play with people's minds. A visual irony is provided in Escher's picture *Relativity* (Figure 10.1). Each of the people in Escher's picture can be seen as having made sense of only the staircase immediately before them; they interpret their world from their own stance. However, when brought together there is an irony, the absence of one universal worldview: the 'helicopter' over-stance is ironic. The picture, like the quote, perhaps creates some confusion in the brain, some decentring, which encourages thought in an attempt to make sense of what has been exposed.

Irony

As Muecke (1982) points out, any word with a history is hard to define. Irony is a good example, and one whose modern meaning is beginning to forget how it differs from paradox and other forms of contradiction. Muecke gets around this problem by dividing irony into at least two types, which he calls observational and instrumental. These may or may not be humorous, but they often cause a mingled effect of pain and amusement. Observational irony is explained using the example of 'is it not ironic that the swimming coach drowned?' The contradiction here is that there is one stance of the expert swimmer

Figure 10.1   *Relativity* by M. C. Escher © The M. C. Escher Company-Holland. All rights reserved. Reproduced with permission (www.mcescher.com).

advising others how to avoid dying in water and yet another stance of wanting to explore circumstances when being an expert swimmer will not be sufficient to avoid drowning. It is ironic because when twisted back on itself opposites are created, and the expert becomes the victim. Instrumental irony, the form of most interest here, is explained by Muecke, who uses the Vietnam War example, 'kill a Commie for Christ today'. Although this only becomes instrumental irony to the extent that different people interpret the phrase in different ways, it was seen by some to turn Christian values back on themselves, others saw little that was contradictory, while yet others simply saw it as an anti-war slogan. Whether one meaning is true and another false is immaterial, more relevant is that there are different stances being revealed. It provides what Muecke calls 'a double exposure … on one plate', 'co-existing, irreconcilable, irrelatable realities'. This is not problematic but rather enlightening. Ironies are not statements that are to be believed, but rather are made to improve understanding.

Another example of irony is the declaration, 'I tell lies'. It can be turned back on itself to reveal an opposite. Is the declaration itself a lie? A moralistic person might choose not to see the irony but rather believe the declaration to be a confession of sin. To us as the audience on this discussion, the declaration may be helping us to understand irony. Irony would therefore appear to be one means of understanding or revealing multiple stances, provided those people with differing interpretations are able to communicate with each other.

Consider the worldlier example of the ironic claim that international trade is a means to preserve unique cultures which otherwise might risk the oppression of poverty. The claim suggests you have to mix with others in order to preserve your own separate identity. This irony opens up at least the perspectives of worldwide trading, and of understanding uniquely distinctive cultures. It may also open up the stance of social phenomena being recursive, of folding opposites back on themselves, and dispelling the stance of linear causality. For a classic text on recursion see Hofstadter (1979).

In the management literature Oswick et al. (2002) pick up on the role of irony as being more stimulating than metaphor as a means for improving our thinking about complex social situations. Metaphors emphasise similarities, as in 'the organisation is like an adaptive organism', while irony attempts to 'decentre' the reader, sometimes in a humorous manner. As an example they revisit Willmott's exposure of the irony of organisational empowerment where those chosen to be empowered are often those who have so far exhibited the highest degree of conformity. Further examples include the idea that anarchy is a form of organisation, as in Joseph Heller's *Catch 22*, and Gibson Burrell's *Pandemonium*. These demonstrate irony as purposefully attempting to decentre the readers initially, to force their reasoning to engage.

Hatch (1997) studied ironic remarks by reflecting on what managers had said immediately before an outburst of laughter. She was particularly interested in the need to be able to appreciate the context around an ironic remark before it appeared humorous. This underscores the locality of knowledge revealed by irony in contrast to a universal stance. One example she uses was when an engineer told the general manager that her department had achieved a quality rating of 51%. The GM's response was 'Fifty one percent? That's Engineering. What would we do without Engineering? We wouldn't have any comedy!' This too can be used to identify contrasting stances. One is that of engineers taking measurement, precision and quantification very seriously. Historians of science such as Cohen (1994) and Latour (1986) emphasise the importance of precision and rigour in the physical sciences. However, as identified in C. P. Snow's two worlds when dealing with self-conscious human beings, such precision needs to be replaced with the insight, imagination and perspective that may come from comedy (Snow, 1993). Precision in quality management practices has the same connotations as calls for precision in beauty. The GM's comments act to refocus physical science criteria towards social enquiry criteria.

It is unclear, however, if irony exists except in language. It may simply be an amusing and novel means of communication. Hatch found more use of irony in some management groups than others. Some groups may simply have learnt to present the everyday as ironic. This may depend on the mood and creativity of people rather than exposing some physical occurrence.

Enquirers might want to seek out ironies as alternative stances that have been revealed. This could include applying a purposeful process of contrasting a 'message' with its 'ends', and identifying when they are in contrast. For example, the 'message' in the Vietnam slogan may have been 'that Christians turn the other cheek' while the 'ends' were actually a war against communism. Another, somewhat classic example is the definition of positivism, which is ironic in that it proclaims that valid knowledge requires empirical testing, a knowledge claim which itself cannot be empirically tested.[6] This approach of contrasting the 'message' with the 'ends' provides a pragmatism for critiquing reports, where the author's advice is turned back on his or her own actions to seek opposites.

Paradox

Quine (1961) defines a (logical) paradox as a conclusion that at first sounds absurd but does have a reasonable argument to sustain it. Social paradox usually means that two opposites appear to exist at the same time, yet each is sustainable through rational argument. Poole and Van de Ven (1989) use the examples of how organisations (like rivers) are both at the same time constant and constantly changing, and how people are both independent and yet dependent on others. The medical profession both relieves suffering and sustains it. Poole and Van de Ven go on to recommend ways of classifying and resolving these sorts of social paradoxes, which suggests that they see paradox as being in need of, and capable of, resolution. Lewis (2000) points out that paradox denotes contradictory yet inter-related elements that seem logical in isolation but absurd when appearing simultaneously. She, however, seems to feel that paradoxes are not to be resolved so much as sought, appreciated and learnt from. Both the Poole and Lewis articles appear to be suggesting that paradoxes are real, discoverable objects. The alternative view considers paradox as being merely a manipulation of language and differing interpretations, but still useful as a way of offering contrasting insights.

Lewis describes paradox (1) as opposing interpretations of particular phenomena, (2) as oppositional thinking, (3) as an aid to understanding divergent interpretations, (4) as perceptual, (5) as becoming apparent through social interaction, (6) as denoting a variety of viewpoints, (7) as residing in the observer, not the observed, and (8) as being a possible outcome of using negatives to define something. She goes on to highlight different approaches for identifying paradoxes. Examples include the analysis of narrative, psychodrama and multi-paradigm. The last involves using opposing epistemologies as a sensitising device for finding paradoxes. In this book the opposite orientation was used. Paradoxes are used to find, explain and justify the existence of alternative inter-pretations which it is thought always exist around any understanding of a complex social phenomenon. Striving to find, remove or work with paradox is thought to be insufficient; rather, paradox needs to be seen as a window through which to appreciate the world creatively.

Arnold (2003) in his discussion on the paradoxical nature of mobile phones opts to use the language of 'Janus faced' after the 'Roman Deity with two faces, cursed and blessed with the necessity of facing two directions at once'. He asserts that mobile phones both make us more liberated yet at the same time leashed, independent yet co-dependent, closer yet more distant to people, private yet public, busy yet available, productive yet consumptive, and boyish yet girlish. Each opposite opens our eyes to a paradox, a new view of the technology. Moreover, like irony, paradox also reveals another stance, that of a world of opposites existing together in harmony.

As with irony, however, it is not clear if paradox exists outside of language. It is fun apparently to present paradoxes but do they physically exist or are they merely a clever means of presentation? Arnold's string of mobile phone paradoxes is perhaps simply an imaginative way of presenting. Invoking James' (1907/1910) advice that when faced with a contradiction one should make a distinction, it seems possible to solve Arnold's paradox by careful definition of words. If 'liberating' means that paradoxes reduce risk, thus allowing new activities, then mobile phones are liberating. Questioning whether paradoxes only exist in language is not to undermine their usefulness in improving our appreciation of a situation.

The Abilene paradox provides another example. This states that sometimes a group will decide collectively upon an action that differs from the preferred action of each of the individual members. Presented like this it is intriguing, because it encourages us to stop and think about our intuitions, to be critical. Critique may be done purposefully by exposing some contrasting stances in the Abilene paradox. One stance revealed may be an assumption that a group should outperform an individual. Armstrong (2000) pre-sents a lot of evidence that small groups do outperform individuals in experimental con-ditions. The other stance this paradox may be seen to expose is one of communication. Small groups appear to be creative because there can be direct, one on one, effective rational argumentation between all members. When interpersonal factors come into play, such as loyalty or being supportive, and override rational argument, then the group can be expected to make irrational decisions. The paradox may also encourage thinking about the behaviour of groups in terms of getting the right balance between collective and individual behaviour. The success of the Delphi method is to ensure individual experiences are correctly tempered by group influence.

Humour

One way of seeing humour is as rapid or playful cognitive reframing (Kelly, 2002). The identification of irony and paradox would seem sometimes to achieve this reframing, but perhaps with less sudden revealing. However, this reframing may also result from an accidental slip, or be driven more by a search for a laughter response than a desire to reveal a meaningful comparison of stances. In her study of social bonding in a group of managers, Hatch (1997) studied their use of irony as humour. She identified ironic episodes as the conversation immediately prior to an outburst of laughter, which reinforces the idea that the decentring nature of irony can be humorous. In an earlier study, Hatch and Ehrlich (1993) concluded that an analysis of laughter could reveal contrasting stances. Humour was often the result of drawing on very contrasting analogies (metaphors). They used a case study of managers discussing security at the entrance to a computer manufacturing company. Humour resulted from shifting the stance of those trying to design an appropriate security system for their firm's reception to talk of gun turrets, chromosome checks and high-security prison routines on entry as well as exit from their factory. The contradiction the humour identifies is that the company wanted to operate a friendly workforce based on trust and goodwill but found it necessary to install a staff security system. Those opting to do overtime were causing the dilemma of putting themselves in a position of suspicion.

Identify the irony or paradox in the following humorous passage.

Jim and Mary were both patients in a mental hospital.

One day while they were walking past the hospital swimming pool, Mary suddenly jumped into the deep end. She sunk to the bottom and stayed there. Jim promptly jumped in to save her. He swam to the bottom and pulled Mary out. When the medical director became aware of Jim's heroic act he immediately ordered him to be discharged from the hospital, as he now considered him mentally stable.

When he went to tell Jim the news he said, 'Jim, I have good news and bad news. The good news is you're being discharged because since you were able to jump in and save the life of another patient, I think you've regained your senses. The bad news is Mary, the patient you saved, hung herself with her dressing gown belt in the bathroom. I am so sorry, but she's dead.'

Jim replied, 'She didn't hang herself. I put her there to dry.'

Source: unknown

The paradox in this joke comes in the humorous 'punch line' which works by suddenly providing an alternative stance on Jim's behaviour: his own rather than that of the 'voiceover'. The voiceover and the medical director's stance seem aligned and dominant at first, but then Jim's is suddenly revealed. If you hold the voiceover's stance then you may be thinking Jim's apparently honest explanation of what he did will now stop him from being discharged. My first take is that the voiceover was encouraging you to accept that the medical director could tell what was true, simply based on his 'God's eye stance' of the patient, using the apparent universal observation of Jim's heroic behaviour in the swimming pool. Hearing Jim's stance on Mary's death totally changes the understanding of Jim, but still only from the voiceover's perspective. The possibility still exists that Jim is sane, that he has a great sense of humour or that he does not want to leave the mental hospital. Moreover, if Jim is insane, then how can we trust what he says about drying out Mary? The passage nicely exposes a myriad of stances, its humour works by luring you into the comfort of thinking there is a universal stance on human behaviour, and then dispelling this by realising two contrasting stances exist.

Clearly humour is a topic of overwhelming complexity (McGhee, 1979), but the reframing type of humour, given that it is so explicitly flagged by laughter, may not only allow the identification of irony and paradox but also provide an example of clashing stances. The same may be said of outbursts of anger. It would therefore seem reasonable to suggest to enquirers to seek occasions of humour or anger and to use these to expose contrasting stances.

Identify the alternative and contrasting stances revealed in the following passage.

> At the turn of the century the insurance companies in the Western world acknowledged the changing economics in families by not allowing parents to insure for the death of their children. Previously, and still for farmers in the Third World, children were an asset because they were free labour. As the wealth of a country increases, and it urbanises, the children turn from an asset to a liability. In modern times the death of a child reduces the financial burden on the parent. You cannot insure against a reduction in costs.
>
> I am perfectly at ease with the selfish gene argument that the main purpose of life is having children, and in providing for those children. It is the genes that are important, not the person. However, as a modern dad I am amused to notice how the role of children has changed in one, my, generation. As a teenager I, proverbially, was a 'strapper' (as in saddling up a horse) for my father but now I am the 'strapper' for my daughters. Increased wealth and excess of food has changed children from an extra pair of hands to help mum and dad around the farm into an expensive cuddly toy. Modern farming methods, including the use of certain

chemicals, mean my children (and me) have to discipline themselves not to eat too much. The increased wealth that follows this food surplus now means dad has a well-paid soft job and has time for hobbies, exercise, volunteer activities and time to play with the kids, all of which were nearly impossible for my grandfather.

I was standing beside my very young daughters watching them eat their breakfast when a friend came in. In that way typical of visiting adults she said to the kids, 'What are you having for breakfast?' They replied, 'Eggs and toast.' 'And what is your father eating for breakfast?' the visitor continued. There was a quiet pause, 'The crusts' one replied.

For me the irony is that the more powerful partner in a parent–child relationship, is the parent who serves the child. It is ironic, rather than a paradox, because most children will see themselves as having to do what their parents want, and the parents see themselves as responsible for the children.

Exercises

1   **Try and identify two contrasting stances in the passage below.**

The house then was on top of a small hill with a 100 metre drive straight down to the passing road. Our cockerel was standing on top of the house which gave it a magnificent view of the surrounding countryside and far up and down the road. One day it started crowing excitedly at something in the far distance. I assumed it was a competitive cockerel that it could just see or hear. Suddenly, the bird jumped down from our roof, ran down our drive and stood right in the middle of the road. All its feathers were up and it looked ready for a fight. A white truck came around the corner and, bang, collected it on the bull-bars. Not quite believing what I had just seen, I wandered down to the road. Sure enough there were the remains of my cockerel scattered over the road. Had it committed suicide? It was clearly waiting for the truck, which it would not have seen until the last moment, as it came around the bend near our house. A few weeks later I too was on the roof about where the cockerel had been. I looked out along the road. Despite the bend near our house, I could see a truck, still tiny in the distance, coming along the road that later passed our house. Of course, in the distance it was only small, which

continued

continued

made me think. Rather than committing suicide I suspect that the cockerel saw the truck in the distance and thought it was small and coming his way. This tiny thing clearly wanted a fight and my guy was up for that. He rushed down the drive to meet the competition head on, only to find at the last second that it had grown considerably since he had spotted it from the roof.

2 **Critique the following passage by making explicit the two contrasting stances.**

Male A: In my house, as the dominant male I make all the important decisions like whether the US should have invaded Iraq or not. My wife merely decides the little things like where I work, where we live, what we eat and when the children go to school.

Male B: In my house, as the man of the house I am responsible for all the strategic decisions and my wife is responsible for all the tactical decisions; however, in the last twenty-five years there have not been any strategic decisions to make.

3 **Critique the following passage by identifying two contrasting stances. Notice the passage was used in the evolution chapter.**

After reading about David Hume's chapter on cause and effect and pondering his comments that we cannot anticipate an 'effect' just from the attributes of something we call a 'cause', I went to have a wash. To my delight my young daughter saw me and ran to join me in the washroom. She climbed up on the small chair we had placed to one side of the washbasin so as to help me have my wash. As I went to turn on the taps she said, 'Do you want hot water.' 'Yes please,' I replied. Her chair was right next to the hot water tap side of the basin. She turned on the tap nearest to her and felt the water, 'It is cold,' she said with a little sigh, 'But don't worry I can make it hot.' 'How?' I said. 'You have to hold your finger under the running water and that makes it go hot!'

4 **Critique the following.**

Start with a cage containing five monkeys. Inside the cage, hang a banana on a string and place a set of stairs under it. Before long, a monkey will go to the stairs and start to climb towards the banana. As soon as it touches the stairs, all of the other monkeys are sprayed with cold water.

After a while, another monkey makes an attempt with the same result: all the other monkeys are sprayed with cold water. Pretty soon, when another monkey tries to climb the stairs, the other monkeys will try to prevent it.

Now, put away the cold water. Remove one monkey from the cage and replace it with a new one. The new monkey sees the banana and wants to climb the stairs.

To its surprise and horror, all of the other monkeys attack it. After another attempt and attack, it knows that if it tries to climb the stairs, it will be assaulted.

Next, remove another of the original five monkeys and replace it with a new one. The newcomer goes to the stairs and is attacked. The previous newcomer takes part in the punishment with enthusiasm! Likewise, replace a third original monkey with a new one, then a fourth, then the fifth. Every time the newest monkey takes to the stairs, it is attacked. Most of the monkeys that are beating it have no idea why they were not permitted to climb the stairs or why they are participating in the beating of the newest monkey.

After replacing all the original monkeys, none of the remaining monkeys have ever been sprayed with cold water. Nevertheless, no monkey ever again approaches the stairs to try for the banana. Why not? Because as far as they know, that's the way it's always been done around here.

And that, my friends, is how company policy begins.

11 Using Reflective Thinking to Critique

Critique the following passage by identifying a decision, how much information went into making the decision and the consequences of making that decision.

Svenssons Falukorv is a meat processing plant in Falun. The plant is highly successful and run as a third generation family firm. Two years ago its current boss, Svensson, the great grandson of the founder, organised its 100 year jubilee. Svensson sells all the falukorv (a low-brow Swedish sausage) that he can produce and has had few concerns over the years. He decided to mark the jubilee with a special advertising campaign. So he went to an advertising agency in Falun.

On entering the agency he was asked: 'OK, then, what is your target group?'

He replied: 'Well … everyone. Everyone eats falukorv, don't they!'

'Mmmm … ', came the reply. 'Are you sure about that?'

'Yes, of course, we sell all we produce in the factory.'

'I see'.

But the agency staff weren't convinced, and decided to conduct a spontaneous, admittedly unscientific, market research survey. All staff from the agency were sent out into the market square in Falun and asked people on their way to lunch what they intended to eat. Then they asked them, if they had initially said they would eat something other than falukorv whether they might consider eating falukorv instead. From this a pattern emerged which, although somewhat puzzling at first, soon became clear.

They then visited additional locations such as school canteens and asked pupils to list their top ten choices for school dinners. Naturally, hamburgers, pizza and fish fingers appeared on the lists, but falukorv was nowhere to be seen. So they returned to Svensson and said: 'You've got problems'.

'Problems?', he said, 'I sell all I produce.'

'Yes, but do you know who you are selling to?'

'To everyone', he insisted for the third or fourth time.

'No!', came the reply, 'you sell to those who are 55 or older. Of course, they eat a lot of falukorv, but they're not going to do so for much longer. You don't understand that you have to adapt your product to the times, because its low-calorie food that's *in* these days, healthy eating and all that … '

This was seen as the devil, but Svensson nevertheless proceeded to reduce the falukorv's fat content, add a few extra spices here and there, increase the proportion of lean meat and eventually succeeded in getting the falukorv on to the school canteen top ten lists at number seven.

(With thanks to Tony Huzzard)

The decision explicitly mentioned in the first paragraph is to have an advertising campaign to celebrate the jubilee. There is no mention of any rigorous process to come to this decision, it seems to have resulted from an analogy of some sort between the jubilee and launching a new advertising plan. The consequences are that the jubilee turned into a major product and market reorientation. These appear to be unintended consequences.

One stance on thinking is that we do not collect information and then make a decision but rather our brains are designed the other way about. We make a tentative conjecture upfront and what we should do next is to think very carefully about the consequences of that conjecture. This stance has a very eminent history, although it seems to have been oppressed by the stance 'don't jump to conclusions until you have collected all the facts' or 'collect the facts before you make a decision'. This chapter will explore the lesser mentioned reflective stance as a means of critique partly because innovative stances may result in innovative critiques. Some of the evidence and reasoning for the reflective stance follows.

John Dewey (1859–1952) seems a good starting place for tracing the origins of the stance. He has been described by some as the most influential philosopher on thinking and education in the twentieth century. Like Schon, he is thought of as a writer on educational philosophy yet both of their works have been seminal to the management literature. Newell and Simon (1972) cite Dewey in their own oft-cited book *Human Problem Solving*, as does Churchman (1971) in his influential book, *The Design of Inquiring Systems*. Simon won a Nobel Prize and Churchman was shortlisted. In more modern times Mintzberg (Mintzberg and Westley, 2001), a seminal figure in the management research literature, directly attributes the rational steps of decision making to Dewey (1910). Dewey spells out the steps (or as he says, constituents) of the reflective stance, which he calls thinking, in his small book, *How We Think*.

Dewey's book starts by defining thinking, which he wants to distinguish from 'daydreaming'. He specifically means focused, purposeful, rational and intelligent thinking. He uses the label 'reflective thinking' in a way we might use 'critical', 'careful', 'considered' or 'deep' thinking today, but importantly he inserts the word 'reflective' apparently in order to emphasise critically reflecting on a prior belief, 'first thought', conjecture or some other 'supposed form of knowledge'.

> Active, persistent, and careful consideration of any belief or supposed form of knowledge in the light of the grounds that support it, and further conclusions to which it tends, constitutes reflective thought …
>
> … it is a conscious and voluntary effort to establish belief upon a firm basis of reasons. (1910, p. 3)

In the second part of the book (which starts at chapter 6) Dewey explains how thinking about 'established belief upon a firm basis of reasons' might be achieved under the chapter heading, 'The Analysis of a Complete Act of Thought'. He starts by presenting three everyday examples of thinking. The first of these is:

> 1.   The other day when I was downtown on 16th Street a clock caught my eye. I saw that the hands pointed to 12.20. This suggested that I had an engagement at 124th Street, at one o'clock. I reasoned that as it had taken me an hour to come down on a surface car, I should probably be twenty minutes late if I returned the same way. I might save 20 minutes by a subway express. But was there a station near? If not, I might lose more than 20 minutes looking for one. Then, I thought of the elevated train, and I saw there was such a line within two blocks. But where was the station? If it were several blocks above or below the street I was on, I should lose time instead of gaining it. My mind went back to the subway express as quicker than the elevated; furthermore, I remembered that it went nearer than the elevated to the part of 124th Street I wished to reach, so that time would be saved at the end of the journey. I concluded in favour of the subway, and reached my destination by one o'clock. (p. 69)

After presenting two other examples Dewey sees some emergent properties in thinking:

> Upon examination, each instance reveals, more or less clearly, five logically distinct steps: (i) a felt difficulty; (ii) its location and definition; (iii) suggestion of possible solution; (iv) development by reasoning of the bearings of the solution; (v) further observation and experiment leading to its acceptance or rejection; that is the conclusion of belief or disbelief. (p. 72)

This appears to be the origin of the idea of what has become the five stages of decision making. Dewey quickly explains that steps (i) and (ii) frequently fuse.

As a flowchart, his steps of thinking might look like Figure 11.1. The feature I am trying to highlight is that a quickly guessed or 'first' solution seems to come *before* the collection of supporting evidence (as reasoning or as empirics). This is why Dewey calls it 'reflective thinking': that is, thinking back on a possible solution. Dewey provides

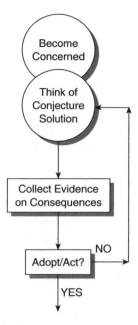

Figure 11.1   Dewey's steps to thinking

synonyms for 'possible solution', first thought' or 'quick idea'. He suggests 'conclusion', 'supposition', 'conjecture', 'guess' and 'hypothesis'.

This idea of placing the solution prior to the thinking will only be novel to those unfamiliar with the ideas behind argumentative enquiry, or of the pattern recognition literature from psychology. Of course, the example provided is very simple, as are the other two examples that Dewey discusses, both of which have the same form. Seeing them as simple examples of thinking might, however, mistakenly open up the possibility of distinguishing reflective thinking as all right for quick everyday decisions, but not for important scientific thinking or project management. This would allow a return to the line of argument that 'jumping to conclusions' needs to be avoided until after some careful consideration of the facts. I would suggest any split between everyday thinking and 'big project' thinking is an error, as big project thinking only includes what is happening in the heads of the individuals involved in a project.

Empirical support

Guindon (1990) provides empirical support for Dewey's examples. He compiled a two-hour protocol analysis of three professional designers who were designing lift (elevator) control software. He struggled to apply Simon's ideas of ill-structured problems to describe the type of trial and error heuristic processes the designers went through to complete an effective design. These designers were well qualified, and very experienced. He concludes:

> This study shows that the early stages of the design process are best characterised as opportunistic. (1990, p. 336)

He found that designers frequently guessed at solutions, and then thought about whether these would work when compared with the requirements. The 'guesses' were accepted, modified or rejected after further thought or testing. There was not a linear process of appreciating the requirements, collecting facts and selection of alternative solutions and then selecting a solution. Although Guindon does not mention Dewey, his description of how his designers solve their problem has similarities to the three examples provided by Dewey. Guindon, however, is concerned that his designers are not following Simon's interpretation of the traditional steps, suggesting this may be because humans only have bounded rationality and are imperfect at reasoning. This assumes Simon's problem-solving algorithms are an idealised form of human problem solving that somewhat inadequate humans should aspire to. Dewey's interest is in how humans think.

Klein (1989) observed the actions of experienced firefighters, nurses, data programmers, soldiers, paramedics and design engineers. He described their problem solving as 'recognition primed': they appeared to observe the problem domain until they recognised a pattern, such as the firemen recognising a particular colour of flames in certain locations. They then knew how to respond, the solution. The task was one of situation assessment not option selection; their efforts went into sizing up the situation. He found that once an option was apparent the experts 96% of the time did not attempt to generate more options in order to make comparisons. Rather they moved on to thinking through whether their conjecture solution would work, or how it would have to be modified to work. Problem solving was not a comparison of alternatives but rather a process of editing their first thought conjectures. This is much what Dewey described above.

Mintzberg and Westley (2001) also noted that some problem solving seems to jump to the solution before any reasoning or evidence has been collected. They call this the 'seeing first' approach (having insights) and contrast it with the traditional step approach which they call the 'thinking first' approach. Part of their critique of the 'thinking first' approach includes the experience that people often seem to have solutions in search of problems, hammers looking for nails. This seems to be a bit like Chalmers' (1982) theory-laden observation. Mintzberg and Westley cite March as characterising problem solving as:

collections of choices looking for problems, issues and feelings looking for decision situations in which they may be aired, solutions looking for issues to which they might be an answer and decision makers looking for work. (2001, p. 90)

Their 'seeing first' approach uses the example of a family seeing a black stool and declaring that this was the solution to the problem of the colour scheme for a new apartment. The apartment is then totally redesigned, successfully, around this stool. The thinking approach would have been to set the colour scheme (plan) and then find furniture and coverings to suit (actions) the plan.

Their third option of 'doing first' thinking aligns with the action learning or practitioner ideas of Argyris and Schon (1978) which suggests that when a problem is identified just guess some action, do it and then think about what happened. Again, the thinking comes after the guessed solution. The doing is expected to provide some experiences to think about. This might be seen as similar to the 'seeing approach' where the action is to 'see' rather than to act.

Philosophers, researchers and experienced management theorists seem to have noticed that humans, when faced with a problem, jump to a tentative solution and then can choose to act to rationalise that conjecture using more critical thinking such as observation, reasoning and experimentation. If the solution is found wanting then it is rejected and another guess evaluated. This is different to the traditional view of rational thinking for solving problems, which required evidence to be collected first, some process of selecting from alternatives, and then a solution is selected. The essential difference is that the reflective, opportunistic, seeing-first approach starts with a conjecture.

Rapid and instinctive response to recognised threatening phenomena does appear to be justifiable in evolutionary terms. Being able to recognise instantly a cliff edge or tiger's face in long grass would seem to give survival advantage. Other examples include rapid hand closure on touching something painful and rapid eyelid closure on exposure to excessive heat. These can be seen as a very instinctive form of problem solving. The rapid instinctive action would seem to involve the brain recognising and responding to what it sees as a danger. However, some readers may want to distinguish this sort of instinctive reaction from 'rational thinking'. Yet, these instant pattern recognition mental responses at least open the door to an approach to thinking that aligns with the idea that the brain very quickly jumps to conjectures; the brain seems to be a rapid recognition organ. In the psychology literature this is often referred to as 'automatic thinking' (Allport, 1954). As Dewey seemed to be suggesting above, reflecting carefully, rationally, scientifically, methodically and systematically upon an intuitive response may be a preferable way of understanding human thinking.

The 'automatic thinking' line of argument from psychology is that the human brain develops schema or mental models to enable us to interpret what we see. This is similar to Kant's a priori, Churchman's perspectival thinking, boundary shifting in systems thinking (Ackoff, 2000), Chalmers' theory-laden observation (Chalmers, 1982) and the ethics literature on framing (Werhane, 2002). At the cognitive level 'vision' can be explained as the brain very rapidly recognising a stream of input through the senses. This is perhaps appreciated by recounting the experiences of adults who undergo eye surgery successfully to correct birth defects causing blindness. In some cases the blindness is caused by a physical fault in the eye that can be corrected by surgery. After the operation, while technically their eye 'works', they are unable to decipher the confusing pattern of colours and light entering their eye. This is apparently not due to some further fault with the optical nerves but rather their brain has no memories, no schemas to use and call upon to interpret the shapes and patterns of light entering their eye.

This may be analogous to how we think. We mix experience as recognised phenomena with new sensory inputs. This reinforces the suggestion that when we think we automatically perceive of the problem from historic schemas or perspective (frames, theories, value, system boundaries) which are likely to be the result of genetic, childhood and broader social influences. This schema of perspective provides an explanation of what is thought about; it gives recognition. Creative thinking can then be defined as suggesting a new recognition, a new perspective on an old problem, one that the others involved in the problem had not considered.

Stigmergy is a term used in the self-organisation biology literature (Camazine et al., 2001) for what is observed in some swarm insects; they seem to react automatically to different physical cues. The experiments usually referred to are those of ants in laboratory Petri dishes. Individual ants have been observed to move sand about in a meaningless random manner until they spot a recognisable shape like a pupa cavity, after which their actions switch to building constructively an extension to this cavity. The shape seems to trigger a responsive action. We can see a similar response in humans who see a person, word, structure, noise or some other phenomenon and respond intuitively from prior experience. An experienced problem solver can therefore be expected to respond rapidly to recognisable situations, jumping to very tentative conjectures.

The conjecture-first approach can also be aligned with writings in the theory of knowledge philosophy. Many philosophers comment that questions are at the beginning of human thought. Crosswhite (1996), in his support for argumentative reasoning, argues that we should really start with the tentative conjectures not the later verbalised question. Children, as well as dumb and deaf people and species without language, all of whom do not have the linguistic device of questioning or know what a question is, can solve problems. They can be expected to become confused as they try and impose a pattern on sensory input. They can also be expected somehow to make sense of these images or noises if only to classify them as 'problematic' by thinking up conjectures (solutions, ideas) that do or do not 'fit'. However, unless these people have rational reasoning skills they might not justify their conjecture in an explicit manner which could aid community learning. Crosswhite, as philosopher, seems to agree that the brain jumps to conjectures based on genetics or experience almost instantly upon receipt of new sensory input; it gives pattern and meaning to these inputs. If the patterns work then there is no problem; conversely if the guessed-at patterns do not seem to fit the sensory input then a problem is declared. Inductive science suggests we should somehow suspend this instant pattern recognition, and rather collect evidence in a state of suspended judgement. Crosswhite feels this is not really possible and repressing this first impression will distort what is seen as relevant evidence. Rather he suggests we acknowledge explicitly what our brains have conjectured and set about confirming or disconfirming it in a methodical manner.

The theory of knowledge literature also suggests this conjecture-first approach in two further and related ways. One way is Popper's (1963) ideas of presenting conjectures for falsification. The other is inherent in argumentative enquiry. Popper's conjectures are meant to be more thought out than instinctive responses, but the basic layout of having an upfront explicit conjecture that needs to be proved to a sceptical audience is the analogous notion. It was intended to be contrasted with the discovery approach of seeking evidence prior to finding some solution. The difference seems to come down mainly to whether you believe that the first thought conjectures can be completely set aside prior to evidence collection and whether *non*-theory-driven observation can be undertaken.

The use of competitive argument and Grootendorst (reasoned debate not quarrelling) as a means of argumentative enquiry, rather than primarily persuasion, now has a number of advocates (Perelman and Olbrechts-Tyteca, 1969; Eemeren and Grootendorst, 2003; Walton, 1998; List and Metcalfe, 2004). As with Popper, the idea is that an advocate declares a knowledge claim to start a competitive enquiry process with a sceptical knowledgeable audience. From this process it is intended that an improved and fully justified knowledge claim emerges. Churchman extends this to seeking participants' perspectives of complex social problems. These perspectives need to be justified to the sceptical audience.

Polya

Another strand of thinking that appears to support the 'conjecture-first' approach to thinking may be drawn from the words of that classic problem-solving text by Polya *How To Solve It* (1945). This booklet is aimed at mathematicians. It provides a suggested methodology to tackle the creative process of solving mathematical and geometric problems. His 'steps' are:

> First. You have to understand the problem.

> Second. Find the connection between the data and the unknown. You may be obliged to consider auxiliary problems if an immediate connection cannot be found. You should obtain eventually a plan of the solution.

> Third. Carry out your plan.

> Fourth. Examine the solution obtained. (p. xvi)

When saying 'understand the problem' Polya seems to mean simply read or observe the problem, a first cut. The argument of this booklet is that while this is being undertaken possible solutions will jump into the reader's head. It is only identified as a problem if none of these tentative conjectures is thought to be viable. Polya provides advice on what to do next with his second step, which advises the need to seek analogous problems that have been solved. He suggests using existing solutions to old problems. This could be described as an act of further appreciating the problem. This is still further elaborated in the third step which Polya states as testing to see if the old analogous solution or at least similar concepts work for the new problem. Polya, who is a well-respected author on problem solving, is therefore not suggesting that solutions come after reasoning about alternatives. Rather, he suggests that you search for a tentative conjecture solution (from an analogous problem) and then think about its usefulness for the current problem. This perhaps does not directly address the issues of prior experiences providing automatic analogies, but it does align with Dewey's ideas and the advice of argumentative enquiry not to seek alternatives and compare them but rather conjecture something that might work, and then think about editing this to fit the problem at hand.

Gilbert (1991) argues 'as perception construes objects, so cognition construes ideas'. He draws on the experimental psychology finding to compare Descartes' ideas on how we move from an idea to a belief with those of Spinoza, opting for Spinosa. Descartes suggests we appreciate ideas in a neutral form and then later decide if they are to be believed or not. Spinosa suggests that the act of appreciating an idea is synonymous with believing it. We then actively have to set about a process of critiquing this belief if we are later to disbelieve it. The evidence Gilbert provides to support his argument is quite extensive, including noting that children have to be taught to be disbelieving, that our language defaults to our beliefs, and it takes more words to state something in the negative. Gilbert reviews the psychology literature on people making decisions when stressed. Their default position is to act as if anything they have been told was correct. Moreover, subjects told the information they were being given was false, when stressed, used it as if they believed it. This all aligns with the human information processing research which shows a general failure of people to seek disconfirming evidence as part of their enquiry strategies. This line of reasoning explains, at the cognitive level, how appreciating a problem is believing it, and how it is appreciated will influence what and how it is believed. How we believe something is likely to affect our initial conjectural solution.

So, in summary, the stance is that when a problem is explained to people they will very quickly jump to a conjecture solution based on prior experience. Rigorous or scientific thinking involves the process of thinking about the consequences of that conjecture. This places a lot of emphasis on how a problem is presented to people and suggests that their conjectured solutions be made explicit earlier rather than later and then be rigorously explored for consequences. This will make good use of prior experience, will make explicit what stance they are using to see the problem and possible solutions and will avoid paralysis by analysis. This paralysis can occur if there is a call for evidence in support of every possible solution to be collected and compared. The end result will be an agreed-upon solution that realises that other solutions may have been found. Moreover, the consequences of the decision have been the main focus.

This then can be used as a stance to critique.

Critique questions

1 What decisions can be identified?

2 How much evidence was collected before the decision?

3 Were all the possible options fully considered?

4 How did the passage deal with the prior perception of those involved?

5 Were the consequences of the decision discussed; were they intended or unintended consequences?

6 Was there an explicit recognition of the need to have formal reflection processes?

Exercises

1   **Critique the following passage. In particular, comment on those involved in thinking through the consequences of their decisions, and their process for insightful reflection.**

Once upon a time, there lived a man named Clarence who had a pet frog named Felix. Clarence lived a modestly comfortable existence on what he earned working at the Wal-Mart, but he always dreamed of being rich. 'Felix!' he said one day, hit by sudden inspiration, 'We're going to be rich! I will teach you to fly!'

Felix, of course, was terrified at the prospect. 'I can't fly, you twit! I'm a frog, not a canary!'

Clarence, disappointed at the initial response, told Felix: 'That negative attitude of yours could be a real problem. I'm sending you to class.' So Felix went to a three-day course and learned about problem solving, time management, and effective communication – but nothing about flying.

On the first day of the 'flying lessons,' Clarence could barely control his excitement (and Felix could barely control his bladder). Clarence explained that their apartment building had 15 floors, and each day Felix would jump out of a window, starting with the first floor and eventually getting to the top floor. After each jump, Felix would analyze how well he flew, isolate the most effective flying techniques, and implement the improved process for the next flight. By the time they reached the top floor, Felix would surely be able to fly.

Felix pleaded for his life, but his pleas fell on deaf ears. 'He just doesn't understand how important this is,' thought Clarence. 'He can't see the big picture.'

So, with that, Clarence opened the window and threw Felix out. He landed with a thud. The next day, poised for his second flying lesson, Felix again begged not to be thrown out of the window. Clarence opened his pocket guide to 'Managing More Effectively,' and showed Felix the part about how one must always expect resistance when introducing new, innovative programs.

With that, he threw Felix out the window – THUD! On the third day (at the third floor), Felix tried a different ploy: stalling. He asked for a delay in the 'project' until better weather would make flying conditions more favorable.

But Clarence was ready for him. He produced a time line and pointed to the third Milestone and asked, 'You don't want to slip up the schedule, do you?' From his training, Felix knew that not jumping today would only mean that he would have to jump TWICE tomorrow. So he just muttered, 'OK, yeeha, let's go.' And out the window he went.

Now this is not to say that Felix wasn't trying his best. On the fifth day he flapped his legs madly in a vain attempt at flying. On the sixth day, he tied a small red cape around his neck and tried to think 'Superman' thoughts. It didn't help.

By the seventh day, Felix, accepting his fate, no longer begged for mercy. He simply looked at Clarence and said, 'You know you're killing me, don't you?'

Clarence pointed out that Felix's performance so far had been less than exemplary, failing to meet any of the milestone goals he had set for him. With that, Felix said quietly, 'Shut up and open the window,' and he leaped out, taking careful aim at the large jagged rock by the corner of the building.

Felix went to that great lily pad in the sky.

Clarence was extremely upset. As his project had failed to fly, he hadn't even learned to steer his fall as he dropped like a sack of cement, nor had he heeded Clarence's advice to 'Fall smarter, not harder.'

The only thing left for Clarence to do was to analyze the process and try to determine where it had gone wrong. After much thought, Clarence smiled and said, 'Next time, I'm getting a smarter frog!'

So Clarence set out to do this. He advertised in the local newspapers and found hundreds of frogs for the void left by Felix. (Because he had wisely left out the exact job requirement from the advertisement.) He selected the ten with the highest fgpa (frog grade point average) and formed a team to accomplish what he had failed to do with Felix.

This team went through the same three day course as Felix and were full of enthusiasm and positive attitude. Feeling that this might be the right time, Clarence told his team what exactly was required of them. It didn't take long for the positive attitude to be replaced by cynicism. However the most out-spoken frog of the lot, Peter (one who had already been marked by Clarence as having distinct upper management qualities), refused to let the apparent difficulty of the task deter him. He quickly formed a sub-committee of five frogs to plan the project and he himself started effort estimation. And he also chose Dave and Sam, both of whom he didn't like very much, to be the first to learn to fly.

Needless to say, Dave and Sam didn't live very long. The flying lessons continued with the frogs joining Felix one by one. When only Peter was left, he tendered his resignation to Clarence, stating low employee commitment as his reason for dissatisfaction with the project and joined another company where he was put in charge of training frogs to fly a Mig-21.

Clarence's company, 'Flighty Solutions', was now finding it difficult to convince its customers that their frogs could fly. The marketing team was told to prepare some aggressive marketing strategies to boost the sagging image of the company. A week later they had a meeting with the top level managers in which they outlined their ideas for an advertising campaign.

Concluding a snazzy PowerPoint presentation, the marketing team said, 'The frogs were in the air from the time they went out of the window to the time they

continued

continued

hit the ground. Technically, therefore, they were flying. From our test records, we found that two frogs flew for 5 seconds, three for 7 seconds, and four for 8 seconds, which gives us an average of 7 seconds' flying time per frog. Our new marketing slogan will be 'Fly for seven seconds with Flighty'.'

The managers were duly impressed and Clarence set out to recruit a new team.

Source: unknown

2   **Critique the following, less humorous, passage using the reflective argument stance.**

Two days in Brussels

Anne is 23 and has worked on the production line at Plas-Products plc., Cwmbran, for about three years. She previously worked in other local factories. She has been in her present job longer than any others and, for the most part, is quite happy there. The money is not too bad, she likes the other girls she works with and there is not too much pressure.

The company manufactures a range of industrial gaskets. Some are moulded plastic and others synthesised rubber and cotton. A range of production methods are used included both injection moulding and the more old-fashioned heated press-moulding system. There are about 250 production workers who work on a double day shift system (6a.m. – 2p.m. and 2p.m. – 10p.m.) and are paid on a piecework system. On average, bonus-earnings are about 20% of total pay. There are approximately 200 female production workers and 50 male production workers. The main union is the TGWU (Transport and General Workers' Union); 90% of the men and 45% of the women are members.

In her spare time Anne plays trombone for the Cwmbran Ladies Brass Band. She is a skilled and highly committed player and this year the band has won through to the finals of the European Ladies Brass Bands competition. In effect, her band will be representing Wales in the final in three weeks' time.

It is Monday morning. Anne is working on the early shift and has been telling all her mates about the band's achievement. They are all pleased and excited for her and some, no doubt, feel a sense of reflected glory. After all, one of them *is* going to Brussels to represent Wales in the European Finals.

John, the shop steward, who works in the adjacent production area, is passing through on his way to the stores. He is informed of the good news and – being a Cardiff City supporter and aware of the symbolic significance of playing in the

European Cup – is similarly enthused. And, ever one to seize an opportunity to improve the image of the union, explains that the union does have some small funds to assist members in pursuit of self-improvement. He says he will put it to the next branch meeting (in five days' time) and see if he can persuade them to vote some money towards her expenses. Anne promises to let him have a note of her hotel and travelling expenses.

It is 10a.m.: tea-break time. Anne has spoken about time off to the chargehand who says she can't see any real problem but says Anne will have to clear it with the Production Manager, Anthony – known as 'the Englishman' – who has worked in the company for about 10 years. Originally employed as a progress-chaser, he reached the his present post two years ago. He has done well – and not through making friends and influencing people.

Anne is a bit nervous – she doesn't often speak to him and feels he has always had a down on her. Nonetheless, she goes to see him and explains that she wants two days' unpaid leave to take part in the finals in Belgium.

Anthony, who has never heard of Brighouse and Rastrick, far less Terry Wogan, is less than sympathetic.

'I'm sorry, but we can't spare you. We've just got a big export order and everyone in your section will have to work their knickers off for the next month if we are going to meet the deadline. So, I'm afraid the answer has got be no.'

Anne, shaken but not stirred, just manages to say: 'But it's the first time we've ever made the finals and I've GOT to go.'

'Maybe, but if people like you didn't take so much time off we wouldn't have so much pressure on the production schedules every time we get a big order.'

'But it's for Wales!', exclaims Anne.

'This export order is for Wales. D'you ever think of that, my dear?'

Exit Anne, backstage; shaken and stirred. She returns to the production line where, tea-break over, everyone is back at work. Despite her tears she manages to explain all that has taken place. Within twenty minutes, through the time-honoured mechanism of 'he said, she said', the whole episode has been told, re-told, elaborated, distorted, dissected, analysed and, most importantly, received universal condemnation.

'But it's not any old competition; it's for Wales.'

'She could have just taken two days on the sick.'

'No one would have been any the wiser.'

'And she would have been paid.'

'What d'you expect; he's English anyway.'

'She's representing all of us.'

'I never did like that Anthony; cold fish.'

continued

continued

'The company could do with the publicity.'

'I wouldn't have said anything. I'd have just gone and told them later.'

And, virtually unanimous from all the production employees: 'It's unfair.'

Once the events had been digested and their apparently blatant injustice firmly established, talk turned to what should be done about it. At about 12 noon, Katie, one of the older production workers – who had been a shop steward some four years previously – went to see John, the shop steward, to ask him what he was going to do about it. John, who not three hours before had been promising the equivalent of a trade union scholarship to finance Anne's Brussels trip, tried to calm things down.

'Now Katie, just wait a minute. We have to think this over. It's not a factory issue. Anyway, we've got three weeks before the final and that gives us time to talk things over with Anthony and Leo, the new Personnel Manager.'

But John was too late.

'No, you just wait a minute. We all feel very strongly about this. Anthony was out of order. He had no right to refuse Anne just like that. We elected you to represent *our* views and that means you have to do as we tell you. We're holding a meeting at the end of the shift and you'd better be there, boyo.'

It is 2p.m. The morning shift have gathered in the canteen. They have informed the afternoon shift as they arrive for work and some 190 female and 35 male production workers are crammed into the meeting. John is trying to control the proceedings from the top of the canteen counter. Katie and a number of other women make stirring calls for action and by 2.25p.m. the workforce has decided to go on strike immediately.

It is 4.30p.m. With some difficulty Leo has arranged a meeting between himself, Anthony, John and Katie who has been propelled into the limelight by her actions.

Leo, recently promoted on the retirement of the previous Personnel Manager, has been with the company for seven years. During that time he has made a good impression, passed his IPM (Institute of Personnel Management) Diploma (part-time at the Polytechnic of Wales, Treforest) and has long planned a number of initiatives to improve industrial relations. He is particularly concerned with improving communication and participation. To this end, he had plans to put forward a scheme to the unions for the creation of Quality Circles in the factory. Through these he hoped to generate an atmosphere of mutual trust and respect, create proper communications, reduce wastage, improve timekeeping and, of course, increase productivity. Anthony, although unenthusiastic about such initiatives, was happy to go along with them.

At the meeting Leo, having been previously uninvolved, took the chair. Anthony repeated what he had said earlier. Anne couldn't be spared over the next month and, in any case, had a poor absenteeism record and didn't deserve any special consideration.

'Her attendance record has got nothing to do with this situation', protested John. 'In any case,' he added, 'if her record is so bad, why did she ask for unpaid leave? Why doesn't she just take the two days without asking?'

Leo got Anne's personnel file and pointed out that while she was regarded as a good employee when at work, she had been absent for 20 days in the previous year, apparently ill.

Katie – while by no means South Wales' answer to Germaine Greer – was outraged at this development.

'What do you mean, "apparently ill?" What do you know about women anyway?'

Source: Tom Keenoy

12 Using Questions to Critique[7]

Use the interrogative pronouns and adverbs, the six Ws – namely, why, when, who, what, where and how – to critique the passage below:

In a certain kingdom, there was a school for the education of princes. Since the King and his court spent much of their time playing chess – indeed, it was called the sport of kings – it was decided that the subject called 'games' should be added to the curriculum of the school. A Wizard was engaged to develop the course. Never having played chess himself, the Wizard was a little uncertain about what to teach in the course. (Only a little uncertain, because his ignorance of chess was outweighed by his strong confidence in his general ability.) Thus, he sought the advice of a colleague in another kingdom and from him received the following communication:

Above all else a course in games should be rigorous and intellectually challenging. We wizards long ago concluded that chess, as actually played, is so complicated that it is impossible to formulate a body of principles and decision rules; these are essential to the rigorous analysis of any subject. We have therefore introduced a few simplifying assumptions. For example, in chess, the pieces move in a bewildering fashion – some forward, some on the diagonal, and some even at a right angle; we have tidied up this confusion by assuming that all pieces move according to the same rule. With such assumptions, we have been able, albeit with great difficulty, to develop a model, a set of principles, and decision rules which are teachable and intellectually challenging. A 700-page treatise describing these is enclosed.

The Wizard was much impressed by the 700-page treatise and used it in his course. He found that it was teachable and that the task of learning this model and solving its problems with the decision rules was indeed rigorous and intellectually challenging, as proved by the fact that good students did well on their examinations, while poor students failed them.

The Wizard maintained an active correspondence with wizards in other kingdoms about the model and its decision rules. In this correspondence, the game was referred to as 'chess' although this was solely for convenience of expression; it was taken for granted that everyone knew that their game was not quite like chess as played in the real world.

Eventually, some of this correspondence came to the King's attention. Although he didn't understand the formulas and the jargon, he did notice that the word 'chess' was mentioned, so he commanded the Wizard to appear before him.

At this audience, the Wizard asked, 'How can I serve you, O King?'

And the King replied, 'I understand that you are teaching the princes how to play chess. I wish to improve my own game. Can you help me?'

'What we call chess may not be exactly like your game, Your Majesty. So, before answering your question, I must analyze the problem. Please describe chess as you play it.'

So the King explained the game of chess. As he did so, the Wizard noted that it had the same physical layout, the same number of pieces, and apparently the same objective as the game he taught in school. It seemed clear therefore that the solution was simply to apply the decision rules for this game although he, of course, did not immediately reveal this fact to the King for he wanted to preserve his reputation for wizardry. Instead, he said thoughtfully, 'I will study the problem and return in ninety days.'

At the appointed time, the Wizard appeared again, carrying a crimson pillow upon which lay a spiral-bound report with a plexiglass cover. It was a paraphrase of the 700-page treatise. 'Follow the rules in this report, and you will become the best chess player in the world,' he said.

The King avidly studied the report, but soon ran into difficulty. He summoned the Wizard again. 'I see reference to kings, and men, and squares, which are familiar terms to me; but what is all this about "jumping," and "double jumping," and "countervailing force" and "suboptimization"? And, where do you mention queens, rooks, bishops and knights?'

'But, Your Majesty, as I have clearly explained in the introduction, it was necessary to simplify the environment a trifle. I doubt that these simplifications lessen the practical usefulness of what I have written, however.'

'Have you by chance watched some chess players to find out?' asked the King.

'Oh, no, Your Gracious Majesty, but I do carry on an extensive correspondence with other wizards. This is better than observing actual practice because it is generally agreed that wizards are smarter than chess players.'

'And, the princes? Are they equipped to play chess in the real world because of what they have learned in your course?'

'No offense intended, Sir, but we wizards do not believe this to be a proper question. The purpose of our course is to teach princes to think – not to prepare them for a mere vocation.'

(Continued)

(Continued)

At this point, the King lost his patience, but since he was a kindly King, he sent the Wizard back to his school room rather than to the dungeon.

Source: Harold Peterson, 'The Wizard Who Oversimplified:
A Fable', *The Quarterly Journal of Economics*, 79(2): 209–211.
© 1965 by the President and Fellows of
Harvard College. Reprinted with permission.

Crosswhite (1996) points out that many philosophers, including Heidegger, Gadamer, Foucault and Meyer, all agree that 'questioning is in every way prior to other ways of acting'. The 'reflective thinking' stance used in a previous chapter may disagree. Foucault writes of the 'serious play of questions and answers' and how 'a whole morality is at stake, the morality that concerns the search for the truth'. It also seems very symbolic that God asks the first question in the Bible while the ancient, yet current, Socratic method of knowledge creation is a questioning methodology. However, where do good questions come from?

Looking to the interrogative pronouns and adverbs in our language seems a reasonable place to start. But, of course, it is not that simple, as your critique of the above passage using them might have highlighted. There would appear to be a few different levels of analysis that could be taken. One may be to concentrate on one character or act in the passage and then use the six Ws to ask questions like why did it happen, who was responsible for what, and so on? A different level of analysis would be to question the moral or scene suggested by the entire passage: why did the King do or not do such, who else could have done such, and so on? Another approach would have been to use the pronouns and adverbs to question the passage as an item: why does the passage exist, who would take heed from the passage, who would not, and so on? The six Ws seem to be a simple enough way to prompt critique questions while not imposing the questioner's agenda on the recipient. However, they can seem insufficient in that they do not suggest an appropriate level of analysis or stance: why what?

The origins of the interrogative pronouns and adverbs in English can be traced back to Aristotle who makes mention of eight circumstances of an act: *quis, quid, ubi, quibus auxiliis, cur, quomodo, quando, circa quid*.[8] These acts are connected, first, with their causes, second with the circumstances and third with the effect or results of the act:

1   **Cause of the act:**

   (a)   **Why did it happen?**

   (b)   **What made it happen?**

   (c)   **Who made it happen?**

   (d)   **With what instruments?**

2   **Circumstances of the act:**

   (e)   **When did it happen?**

   (f)   **Where did it happen?**

   (g)   **How did it happen, in what manner?**

3   **Result of the act:**

   (h)   **What happened?**

Aristotle collected these together as:

> A man may be ignorant, then, of who he is, what he is doing, what or whom he is act-ing on, and sometimes also what (e.g. what instrument) he is doing it with, and to what end (e.g. he may think his act will conduce to someone's safety), and how he is doing it (e.g. whether gently or violently).

The pronouns were further developed by the thirteenth-century Danish theologian Augustine of Dacia, for use as a meditation to analyse the deviation of the soul from the path of righteousness.[9] However, possibly the best-known reference to the interrogative pronouns comes from Rudyard Kipling, Nobel Prize winner in Literature, in his poem from *The Elephant's Child* in the *Just So Stories*:

> I Keep Six Honest Serving Men
>
> I keep six honest serving-men (They taught me all I knew);
> Their names are What and Why and When, and How and Where and Who.
> I send then over land and sea, I send them east and west;
> But after they have worked for me, I give them all a rest.
> I let them rest from nine till five, for I am busy then.
> As well as breakfast, lunch and tea, for they are hungry men.
> But different folk have different views; I know a person small –
> She keeps ten million serving men, who get no rest at all!

She sends 'em abroad on her own affairs,
from the second she opens her eyes –
One million Hows, two million Wheres, and seven million Whys!

Source: Kipling, 1902. Reprinted with permission from
AP Watt Ltd on behalf of The National Trust for
Places of Historic Interest or Natural Beauty.

There seem to be far more cases of these interrogative pronouns (and adverbs) being recommended than researched. Applications span many different disciplines, perhaps illustrating the versatility and generalisability of such a simple scheme. A typical example is Purcell (2000), who writes about value engineering which is a method of determining how to perform a function at the least cost possible. He suggests the use of Kipling's six honest men when evaluating cost/function relationships, citing an example of designing an advanced transponder in an aircraft. Purcell suggests that once the cost/function relationship is established the contractor then tries to develop ways in which to perform the same function at the lowest possible cost without loss of reliability. The principal tools in this activity are the questions: What is it? Why is it needed? Where is it used? Who or what uses it? How is it used? How often is it used? Who is responsible for maintaining it? What does it do that something off the shelf wouldn't do as well? What materials is it made of, and are there cheaper materials that would do the same thing? But, notice how he is indirectly recommending a 'needs or use' stance to be attached to the pronouns and adverbs.

Bowles and Parkinson (1995) suggest using the interrogative pronouns as a starting point in a financial auditing exercise. They believe the answers to the pronouns will give clues as to the right questions to ask during the audit. Mason (1994) outlines the use of the pronouns as a thinking tool in the preparation of a language course in a health care environment. Dawson (2000) suggests the use of the pronouns in the process of power negotiating. He notes that he likes the question 'Why?' even though it can easily be seen as accusatory: 'Why did you do that?' Dawson suggests softening the question by rephrasing it using 'What?' instead of 'Why?': 'You probably had a good reason for doing that. What was it?' Watzlawick et al. (1967) suggest a rule of thumb: Where the why? If a behaviour remains obscure, the question 'What for?' can still supply a similar answer. Dawson also suggests using the six honest men to find out what you need to know.

Whetten (1989) discusses the use of the interrogative pronouns when evaluating and reviewing journal papers for publication in the *Academy of Management Review*. Kepner and Tregoe (1997) use a process to create a problem statement in terms of deviation from normal behaviour. Once the problem is defined they use their problem analysis process to describe the problem in detail by specifying it in four dimensions: what – the identity of the deviation; where – the location of the deviation; when – the timing of the deviation; and extent – the magnitude of the deviation. It seems the pronouns are also frequently used in the courtroom. Lisnek and Oliver (2001) offer advice to trial lawyers on communication techniques for the courtroom. Carson (2003) suggests that a unifying systems model must clearly explain how, why, where and when. Why is about values and beliefs; how is about capabilities; what is about behaviour; and when/where is about boundaries.

Jensen (1978) is one of the few authors who tries to formalise the interrogative pronouns into a problem-solving method called *dimensional analysis*. It defines the pronouns in terms of five dimensions, which it calls: substantive dimension; spatial dimension; temporal dimension; quantitative dimension; and qualitative dimension.

The spatial dimension. ('Where?')
The spatial dimension questions are based on: local or distant (is it merely local or are their some remote influences?); particular location(s) or within a location (recognise the exact area concerned); isolated or widespread (is the problem isolated or linked to several other problem areas?).

The temporal dimension. ('When?')
The temporal dimension questions are based on: long-standing or recent (which parts are new and which are old?); present or impending (is the problem happening or looks as though it may happen?); constant or ebb-and-flow (is the problem always there, irregular or cyclic?).

Quantitative. ('How much?')
The quantitative dimension questions are based on: singular or multiple (is there a single cause or are there many?); many or few people (how many people are affected by the problem?); general or specific (is the problem applicable to a broad category or very specific sub-area?); simple or complex (are there several elements to the problem with complex interactions?); too much or too little (appears as a shortage or surplus).

The substantive dimension. ('What?')
The substantive dimension questions are based on: commission or omission (doing something wrong, or failing to do something); attitude or deed (is it necessary to change attitudes or practices?); ends or means (is the irritant we see the actual problem or merely a symptom of it?); active or passive (active threat or source of irritation); visible or invisible (is the problem masked, e.g. covert human relations issues?).

Qualitative. ('How serious?')
The qualitative dimension questions are based on: philosophical or surface (is it an issue with deep values or surface practicalities?); survival or enrichment (is it a live-or-die issue, or one to do with managing quality?); primary or secondary (what priority does the issue have, top or bottom?); what values are being violated (to what degree are they being violated?); proper or improper values (not all values should be honoured).

Interestingly, this dimensional analysis version of the interrogative pronouns does not seem explicitly to include 'why', which is a question often considered central to scientific research.

The Matter Model

Yardley and Kelly (1995) developed what they call the *Matter Model* while arguing that we are in danger of asking questions based on what we already know. To avoid this, the Matter Model questions are designed to be asked of passages. This makes it particularly relevant to the task of this critique book, intending to reveal insights from retrospection. The Matter Model suggests seven dimensions:

when (a time-based question that reveals wants and desires in the passage);
which (a space-based question that reveals relationships in the passage);
who (a space-based question that reveals relationships in the passage);
where (a space-based question that reveals relationships in the passage);
what (a question about what matters that reveals values and beliefs in the passage);
how (a question about action that reveals movement in the passage); and
why (a question about balance that reveals reasons from the passage).

Symbolic Logic Model

Another approach to the interrogative pronouns exists, one which expands the 'what' question. Carroll (1939) proposed:

Theorem: What would happen if you did?
Inverse: What would happen if you didn't?
Converse: What wouldn't happen if you did?
Reverse: What wouldn't happen if you didn't?

Overduff and Silverhorn (1996) use the metaphor of a pair of gloves to describe symbolic logic, suggesting the gloves could be worn normally (theorem), one inside out worn on the left hand (inverse theorem), and one inside out worn on the right hand (converse theorem). The non-mirror-image reverse of the glove would include everything in existence other than the glove.

Critique questions

The above discussion appears in Table 12.1 which expands the intent behind the different pronouns. However, this does not remove the problem mentioned at the

Table 12.1   Interrogative pronouns

Interrogative pronoun	Dimensional analysis	Aristotle	Matter Model	Hookin's summary
Why? Why not?		Cause of an action	A question about balance that reveals reasons, explanations, theory, viewpoint	Philosophical
Where? Where not?	Spatial	Circumstances of an action	A space-based question that reveals relationships	Spatial
Who? Who not?		Cause of an action	A space-based question that reveals relationships	Identify
When? When not?	Temporal	Circumstances of an action	A time-based question that reveals wants and desires	Temporal
How serious?	Qualitative	Circumstances of an action	A question about action that reveals movement	Qualitative action
How much?	Quantitative	Circumstances of an action		Quantitative action
Which?			A space-based question that reveals relationships	See who or what
What? To what end? What happened?	Substantive	Cause of an action Result of an action	A question about what matters that reveals values and beliefs	Behavioural
What would happen if you did?				Interpretive
What wouldn't happen if you did?				Converse interpretive
What would happen if you didn't?				Inverse interpretive
What wouldn't happen if you didn't?				Reverse mirror image interpretive

beginning about level of analysis when critiquing passages. Perhaps the critiquer simply has to decide to ask the questions of the people or things in the passage, the moral or message of the passage, or the passage as a whole.

Exercise

1 Critique the following speech using the interrogative pronouns and adverbs.

It started out innocently enough. I began to think at parties now and then to loosen up. Inevitably though, one thought led to another, and soon I was more than just a social thinker. I began to think alone – 'to relax,' I told myself – but I knew it wasn't true. Thinking became more and more important to me, and finally I was thinking all the time. I began to think on the job. I knew that thinking and employment don't mix, but I couldn't stop myself.

I began to avoid friends at lunchtime so I could read Thoreau and Kafka. I would return to the office dizzied and confused, asking, 'What is it exactly we are doing here?' Things weren't going so great at home either. One evening I had turned off the TV and asked my wife about the meaning of life. She spent that night at her mother's.

I soon had a reputation as a heavy thinker. One day the boss called me in. He said, 'Skippy, I like you, and it hurts me to say this, but your thinking has become a real problem. If you don't stop thinking on the job, you'll have to find another job.' This gave me a lot to think about.

I came home early after my conversation with the boss. 'Honey,' I confessed, 'I've been thinking ...'

'I know you've been thinking,' she said, 'and I want a divorce!'

'But honey, surely it's not that serious.'

'It is serious,' she said, lower lip aquiver. 'You think as much as college professors, and college professors don't make any money, so if you keep on thinking we won't have any money!'

'That's a faulty syllogism,' I said impatiently, and she began to cry. I'd had enough. 'I'm going to the library,' I snarled as I stomped out the door.

I headed for the library, in the mood for some Nietzsche, with a PBS station on the radio. I roared into the parking lot and ran up to the big glass doors ... they didn't open. The library was closed! To this day, I believe that a Higher Power was looking out for me that night. As I sank to the ground clawing at the unfeeling glass, whimpering for Zarathustra, a poster caught my eye. 'Friend, is heavy thinking ruining your life?' it asked. You probably recognise that line. It comes from the standard Thinker's Anonymous poster.

Which is why I am what I am today: a recovering thinker. I never miss a TA meeting. At each meeting we watch a non-educational video; last week it was 'Caddyshack.' Then we share experiences about how we avoided thinking since the last meeting. I still have my job, and things are a lot better at home. Life just seemed ... easier, somehow, as soon as I stopped thinking.

Now that makes you think, doesn't it?

Source: unknown

13 Using Multiple Stances to Critique

The previous chapters each presented one different way of critiquing a passage. Appreciating the viewpoint a critique comes from is thought to be important training in thinking. Reflection on, and development of, that viewpoint is also thought to be important in order to provide a more considered, complete and systematic critique. The next stage is to encourage critiques from multiple viewpoints. This is not just another exercise in mental gymnastics but a means of building up your own ethics. Appreciating that complex social situations can be seen from numerous equally valid viewpoints is perhaps the starting point for racial, cognitive and social tolerance.

The passage below is larger than has been used in previous chapters but at least it is humorous. It is about presenting medical research findings to a troublesome audience. The passage can itself be seen as an ironic critique on defending research findings from a 'language games' viewpoint. It will be used to demonstrate the provision of multiple critiques.

Factifuging (extracts from)

We have all listened with horrified fascination to the undermining or demolition of a sound piece of research – particularly when it is our own. We may sense that the arguments are false but be unable to detect wherein the fallacy lies.

    Time and again in the short history of science, ideas that were 'conclusively disproved' have later been recognised to be not only correct, but of stunning significance. The heliocentric theory of the immediate universe, the airplane, and even such trivial but useful inventions as the disposable diaper, were each in turn derided and shown to be impossible. It was only the faith of the bold investigator that enabled him to persist in the face of overwhelming evidence that what he was doing was logically and 'factually' impossible. How many vital discoveries that might have benefited the entire world have been lost because the discoverer was not equipped to contend with the reactionary forces marshalled against him! The propounder of a new invention, technique, or hypothesis can almost invariably determine intuitively whether or not his idea is correct.

To help the oppressed author or speaker a list of some of the most successful techniques for defending the intuitively correct position against contradictory data, irrefutable logic, and opposite conclusions would be invaluable. This can be served by the Art of Factifuging.[10]

DISTRACTING

Joking

A cleverly told story can draw the sting of many a serious attack. Some point in the counterattack should 'remind me of a story'. Members of the audience are left in a favourable frame of mind toward the provider of the anecdote (which they may add to their own repertoires). More important, they are also left with the impression that even if the point of the attack still is evident, it really is something like the joke – and therefore not to be taken too seriously.

Individualising

When the mass of statical evidence is so overwhelming as to be incontrovertible, you should attempt to set it aside rather than dispute it: imply that 'All this may well be true but the case in point throws into question the usefulness of a statistical conclusion'. You should then relate in considerable detail (and with a sense of awe at the miracle accomplished) the record of an individual case or experiment which confirms your own approach. If the manoeuvre is properly executed, the audience is left with the impression that there must be something wrong with either the statistics themselves or the use of statistical techniques in this particular instance.

Visual-aiding

Properly speaking this is not a separate technique, since it must be utilised as an adjunct to one of the other approaches but its importance warrants this inclusion. Visual-aiding has become popular recently, with frequent use of cartoons, simple bar graphs in colour, and brief movies of attractive secretaries, illustrating material which has little or no pertinence to the subject. In the *mores* of our scientific culture

(Continued)

(Continued)

one always 'suspends judgment' until the person attacked has had the opportunity to reply. The introduction of such *inconsequentia* forces the audience to defer a decision, in the expectation that the material being presented will ultimately be shown to have relevance. The longer the period intervening between the attack and the reply, the more likely that the strength of the assault will be diluted. Not infrequently, the very point of the attack is lost in following irresistible visual or auditory aids.

The negative side of this technique has not been recognised and its use to date has been purely accidental. It is based on the use of tables, graphs, or other figures which the attacker has previously published. Your selection from his articles of illustrations which are out of context, or unrelated to the point at hand, creates the impression that your antagonist is irresponsible, obtuse, or both. Also, presenting his material at approximately one-half of the original size, and arranging to have the slide slightly blurred, shows that he is a mere collector of data who cannot present his work clearly, and therefore is probably somewhat blotchy in his thinking.

Etymologising

To distract the audience by this technique, you take the currently accepted use of the word and show that it is derived from some related but different meaning.

For illustration, if the point of attack involves the concept of 'personality', you can quite readily confuse the issue by pointing out that the word is derived from *persona*, the mask worn by Greek actors. *Personality* thus refers not to the true individual but to the appearance or face he wishes to present to the world. Or take the word *snob*, an abbreviation of *sine nobilitate* (s. nob.), first used in reference to scholars at the English universities who were not members of the nobility. Thus, the conventional usage of *snob* as one who feels he is better than other people can be shown to 'really mean' that it is one who feels that he is less accepted than others.

With the aid of a dictionary of word origins, you can become adept at showing that everything is either itself or its opposite.

Greeking

Greeking is by no means limited to the Greek language, although Greek and Latin form the backbone of this distraction. *Pari passu et mutatis mutandis*, there is always an expression to clarify your own *Weltanschauung*. This should not be overdone because, as Clauberg of Groningen has so aptly put it, '*Entia non sunt multiplicanda praeter necessitatem*'. Currently, Russian folk proverbs and Japanese *haiku* are becoming popular. As with post-traumatic amnesia, the 'shock wave' introduced by such unexpected, but apparently logical, foreign phrases not only disturbs the material which follows, but also upsets the acceptance of what was previously presented.

Apodicting

This is the art of issuing sentialtious statements which presumably are self-evident and therefore not in need of experimental data. If your opponent protests that the example you have used while individualising is atypical, you should apodictise to the effect that 'it is the extreme which justifies the mean'. By the time anyone has this figured out the point scored against you is lost, because 'a reasonable doubt' has been raised as to the validity of the criticism. It is best to avoid clichés such as 'figures don't lie but liars will figure', or 'one should use a treatment while it still works', since these are likely to have a negative effect and convince the listener that the rebuttal is without originality, vigour or point.

A separate paper on 'The Art of Apodicting' is in preparation. This deals in considerable detail with such techniques as the proteron-hysteron – e.g., 'Don't put the horse before the cart', 'Rolling moss gathers no stones', 'I'd rather be President than right'. Other sections deal with the identity phenomenon: 'Don't make molehills out of molehills.' 'No matter which any says, medicine is medicine.' The beginner should spend a few hours inventing relevant apodictive statements and memorising them, so as to have a basic supply available for his own specialty. The subject is too extensive to be done justice in this essay – and to do it adequately we must do it adequately.

Diverting

Probably the major technique of distraction is to systematically lead the discussion away from a dangerous area. This you can do by saving a few of your most effective and telling points for the rebuttal, and introducing them with the remark 'Now to deal with the point that Dr. Itzenplitz has raised' – proceeding then to give your own material which is unrelated to the criticism just presented. It is always understandable that to develop your answer fully takes more time than was allotted to you, and 'were there but world enough and time' you would successfully have answered the points that *were* raised – just as you succeeded in answering some of the points that were not raised.

DENIGRATION

Neutralising and Anti-neutralising

The careful selection and insertion of certain key words innocent in themselves can have a most salutary effect. These words are designated as 'neutralisers' because they serve to render ineffectual, meaningless, or to throw into question the phrase or sentence which follows them. Refer to the major point or procedure of

(Continued)

(Continued)

your antagonist and insert immediately before his key phrase 'reputed', 'so-called', 'presumed', 'attempted', 'supposedly', 'claimed', and so on. At the same time, anti-neutralising words can be used in contrast, to strengthen your own argument, as in 'the clear and incontrovertible evidence from our statistically controlled studies'.

Mispronouncing

The obvious application is to proper names. If your antagonist has stressed the researches done by T. P. H. Smith you should then make reference to the work of 'P. D. Q. Brown or whatever his name is', implying that the reference is remote and esoteric, and therefore carries little weight. You can also 'mispronounce' entire experiments by beginning correctly with what was done, and ending very sketchily, saying 'or whatever it was that he did', since it obviously is not a piece or work that any scholar of the subject would regard seriously.

Old Hatting

This type of denigration depends largely on the German literature, both real and imaginary. It is a known fact that the Germans have already done everything, and if a reference is not immediately handy it is always possible to refer to an article which must have been done, even though you yourself may not have seen it. There is always someone in the audience who will think he has read the article and will gladly furnish you with an author or a journal. It is well to have available a list of some of the more remote and discontinued periodicals, and occasionally it is helpful to refer to such apocryphal periodicals as the *Archiv für Gierschift und Krankschaft*. With this technique, you can belittle what might otherwise be damning testimony by pointing out how this identical issue was raised 28 years ago by Herr Doktor X and successfully refuted by Professor Y.

Faint-praise Damning

This is the rug-pulling technique whereby your opponent is complimented for something he has said or done, and as he drops his guard the knife is slipped in. For instance, 'that was a wonderful *idea* and it is too bad that it was not just a little better implemented'. Or 'the instrumentation developed for this project is truly outstanding, and if the design itself had been thought through just a little more one might properly have called it a work of genius'. One of the neatest rejoinders is 'everything you say is perfectly true and it is brilliantly put. If it were relevant to our discussion I would be in great difficulties, and for my own sake I am glad it is not'.

BIBLIOGRAPHISING

Pingponging

If there is a well-known study which is in contradiction to your own it is wise to mention this, as the audience may know of it already, or a discussant may bring it up. The reference should, however, be submerged in a ping-pong rally. This consists of quoting one study on your side, then a study in disagreement, and then another study which agrees with you, and then to slip in the bothersome results. Follow by at least one more ping and pong, so that the impressions is created that it is 'just one more' investigation.

Pseudo-equalising

In the ping-pong method just referred to there must exist at least rough equality in the number of studies pro and con. A serious problem is created when only one or perhaps two studies agree with you, and an overwhelming number disagree. In these circumstances avoid stating who is on what side and remark: 'there have been excellent studies done by A, b, C, d, E, f and G but with conflicting results,' or 'there has been disagreement among investigators.' ...

SCUTTLING THE SUBJECTS

Latent-overting

So far, this device is useful mainly if the subjects are classified according to psychological factors, or if psychological factors are relevant to the results. If the subjects are designated as white, healthy, heterosexual males, you can raise the question as to whether they may not be latent homosexuals. If the subjects are overt practising Lesbians, you can raise the issue as to whether they are not latent heterosexuals. Passivity is obviously latent aggression, just as overt aggression is evidence of latent passivity. With this form of jujitsu you can often turn an apparent attack to the support of your own thesis. Now that latent viruses have been proposed as cryptic causative agents in cancer, the technique is acquiring wider usefulness.

Biassing

It is fortunate that the subjects have to be something. Whatever they are can always be used as the basis for raising a doubt about the validity of the work. For example,

(Continued)

(Continued)

subjects have to be either volunteers or non-volunteers. In the former instance they are odd, since they volunteer to take part in the research, and in the second they are resentful and thus biased, because they were forced to participate. They either have, or have not, reached a certain educational level; they either are, or are not, males; they must have reached a certain chronological age; they have to have been brought up in one or another part of the country. Whatever it is that they are, or are not, can be used as the basis for claiming probable or possible bias in their responses.

Uncontrolling

Just as the design of the experiment must always contain uncontrolled items, the same is true of the selection of subjects. It is quite effective to point out that neither the experimental design *nor* the selection of the subjects was completely controlled. ...

FUNDAMENTALING

When it becomes necessary to derail the argument, fundamentaling is the technique par excellence, but it should be used only once in a given setting. When you are caught dead to rights, and it is important to have your opponent appear to be converted to your point of view, you offer a series of propositions which are irrefutable. Point out that you both believe in the value of good treatment, that you both are concerned with high intellectual honesty, that you are both interested in empirically demonstrating any theoretical conjectures, and that you may even be using the same kind of apparatus or technique. Ergo, you are completely agreed on fundamentals, and it is only some minor and adventitious detail which separates you from complete unanimity. In point of fact, then, your opponent actually agrees with what you are saying but has probably only expressed it somewhat differently.

The converse of this technique is valuable when a relatively unknown discussant has got hold of some nasty little fact, of which he won't let go, and which upsets your whole position. Then the argument should be shifted to a ground on which you are much stronger or where only opinion prevails. He has used subjects over the age of 35 and yours are all below that age; his graphs are made with red lines and yours are made with black; he has used a Zeiss microscope and you have used an American Optical Company model; hence, your fundamental approach to the problem is irreconcilable and as long as you disagree about such basic points there is really no object in even discussing the present fact, since it eventually goes back to much more important differences which would first have to be settled.

NOTHING BUTTING

Koehler many years ago pointed out the existence of 'nothing but' theories in which all phenomena are reduced to a basic theoretical postulate, with no demonstration of how, or to what degree. Thus, painting is 'nothing but smearing faeces'; hoarding money is 'nothing but anal retentiveness'; a desire to have a moment's quiet is 'nothing but oral passivity', whereas enjoyment of activity is 'nothing but oral aggression'. Any position opposing yours is 'nothing but' another way of stating what you have already said, or something so monstrous as to be inconceivable.

NOMIFYING

Since we exist in a universe which is 99% inexplicable, we have retained our sanity by naming things which we cannot understand. This removes the terror and mystery from them so that they can be handled with contemptuous familiarity. The same service can be used to reduce the discomfort arising from information provided by your antagonist. Simply provide or invent a name which sounds as though it should be familiar, and no further explanation is needed. Rather than question the technique of collection, the methodology, or the data, you can also out-interpret the sceptic. If the statistics show an interesting piling up in a place which is counter to your thesis, it is incumbent upon you to point to this and say, 'It is interesting to see this curious distribution – of course it is nothing but a "Poisson shower".' If asked later what a Poisson shower is, you simply reply 'a curious piling up of cases as was illustrated in today's data'.

... MORAL

Factifuging, like vermifuging, is an unpleasant but sometimes necessary task and it should be done with clean and sanitary techniques, and with the least possible destruction of healthy tissue.

Source: N. S. Kline (1962), 'Factifuging' in *The Lancet*, 1396–1399. © 1962, with permission from Elsevier.

An attempt will now be made to generate critique statements from this factifuging passage using many of the stances mentioned in previous chapters. Of course they are my personal response, yours may be very different.

Argument

1   The object or phenomenon under consideration can be seen as the presentation of research findings.

2   The perspective being taken is an ironic one around language.

3   The argument in the passage is therefore something like that in research findings' seminars the distinction between reasoned argument and rhetorical bluff is sometimes rather thin.

4   In research findings' presentations audiences should be careful to distinguish the real facts from claims based on insincere language games.

5   Presentations of research findings will always include some insincere language games to persuade the audience not to expect the choice of language to be neutral.

System thinking

6   The system identified from the passage is the one that *transforms* private knowledge into public knowledge.

7   A researcher may believe he or she knows something, such as the cure for an aliment. In order for this to become scientific or publicly accepted knowledge the researcher has to persuade a knowledgeable, and hopefully sceptical, international audience that the cure really does work.

8   The persuasion system has various *elements*, including evidence, explanations, laboratories, reputations, journals, books, conferences, seminars and schools of thought.

9   The *purpose* of the system is to force the claimant, the researcher, to fully justify his or her knowledge claim thus hopefully filtering out the medical quackery.

10   The *stakeholders* include the researchers, the knowledgeable audience, the lay audience, politicians and the ethicists.

11   The *boundary* of the system is not to include spiritual matters, some post-modern definitions of knowledge, advertising claims and politicians' promises.

12   The passage raises the issues of whether irony and humour are part of this knowledge justification system. Typically they are not.

13   Increasingly irony is being seen as a learning tool even for medics.

14   Shifting the systems perspective, the system invoked by the passage could also have been seen as:

15   a sub system of science,

16   the design of human enquiry,

17   the rules of public argument, and

18   a secular humanism education system.

Pictures

19   The picture the passage reminded me of is Foucault's famous 'This is not a pipe' picture of a pipe (Foucault, 1973). It is a picture not a pipe.

20   The passage emphasises our confusion between the object and how we appreciate the object.

21   The object under consideration in the factiguging passage is research presentations.

22   The means used to appreciate this object is humour, language games, not a picture.

TO&P

23   The technical perspective (T) is that an archetypal mathematician could see the passage as an example of the failure of everyday language for the creation of scientific knowledge.

24   Logic and mathematics, he or she might claim, is not open to such manipulations of persuasion, where mathematical proofs are required to follow indisputable logical steps to a proof.

25   This is a rather naïve view of both mathematicians and the absence of interpretation in mathematical proofs but may serve to highlight one possible perspective on the passage.

26   In this perspective the irony in the passage is seen as mere fun, not what self-respecting scientists would or should actually do.

27   The organisational perspective (O) might be provided by a politician, who would perhaps be a lot more sympathetic about the need for a little spin on important research findings if they are to attract competitive investment funding.

28   A politician would appreciate that good findings do not and should not speak for themselves; they have to be passionately argued for.

29   The classic example may be the laws of evolution which after 150 years of vigorous debate are still not fully accepted by the wider community.

30   The end justifies the means.

31   The politician could be expected to argue, as Aristotle does in *Rhetoric*, that convincing people involves more than pure logic.

32   Clarity of communication, the credibility of the source and the sort of image invoked in interlocutors' minds are seen as some of the necessary actions to make a persuasive case.

33   The personal perspective (P) might be provided by a psychologist who might use the passage to reflect on the personality of the author.

34   The irony could be seen as an intelligent, well-educated person's rebellion against authority.

35   Suggests a child who was humiliated by an authority figure deriding his or her genuine efforts to learn using petty etymological issues.

36   There are also hints of split personalities in irony.

37   The genuine person is in search for truth and meaning.

38   The ironic cloak provides another personality who uses language games to defend against small-mindedness.

Concern solving

39   The idea of the concern solving method is to review apparent person-less problems as the concerns of particular interested parties.

40   This factifuging passage is already written at a personal level, being about people and their possible response to social pressure.

41   The problem has already been subjectified.

42   To be seen as a problem rather than as someone's concern, it should have been written as if it was about the need for tight, well-crafted, logical writing in science. Irony and metaphor would be seen as 'flowery', humour as inappropriate, use of Greek and Latin as appropriate, and insincere referencing as scandalous.

43   How could the concern be moved from the personal to the third party? For example, perhaps the concern of people needing to use 'non-scientific' means to present research findings could be presented as a 'systems failure'.

44   It is not the oppressed author's fault that he or she has to resort to such games to get his or her important message out, it is the system's fault.

45   The system may be the seminar circuit, or the scientific publication system or perhaps the academic careers system.

46   Improving the publication system may stop this sort of individualism from occurring.

Observation and experience

47   The distinction between reasoned argument and rhetorical bluff is sometimes rather thin.

48   The supporting evidence provided in the passage is neither predicate logic, mathematical proof nor the result of a controlled laboratory experiment.

49   There is a lot of general reasoning, numerous examples and analogies which draw on the readers' past experiences.

50   The past experiences may be from 'observations' (experiences, empirics) while attending research findings' seminars or from everyday speech, debate and quarrels.

51   Should this experiential evidence be discarded as invalid?

52   Would a series of laboratory experiments recording the audience's response with or without insincere language games make a more valid contribution to knowledge?

53   Perhaps more convincing would be the inclusion of the other means of justification for the argument.

54   There is no explanation why the distinction between reasoned argument and bluff is so thin, so the passage does not provide any guidelines for identifying the distinction, except to be suspicious.

55   A voice is denied to experts on reasoned argument but it is guessed they could be very sanctimonious about the factifuging passage as providing unethical advice.

56   Adding alternative explanations may make the evidence presented in support of a passage more convincing.

Metaphor

57   The root metaphor of the factifuging passage, I suspect, goes past humour, past language, past persuasion to 'facts'.

58   The irony in the passage is perhaps because it recommends the use of non-factual language games to defend scientific 'facts'.

59   A fact is implicitly something that is true, like a particular measurement.

60   A fact is something not being argued about at present.

61   Irony can be considered to be the opposite of metaphor.

62   A metaphor is about similarities; a research findings' seminar is (like) legal argument in court.

63   Irony is about dissimilarities; a research findings' seminar is *pure self-advertising!* (Suggesting it shouldn't be.)

64   Irony requires extensive context and a full appreciation of the norms of those involved.

65   The self-advertising comment may not be irony to some political public relations advisers but would be to scientists who took their work very seriously.

Contradictions

66   Irony must then also be about contradiction: saying one thing and meaning another. 'The war in Iraq really sorted out the terrorism problem!'

67   What were the underlying tensions that resulted in the creation of the factifuging passage?

68 The tension between the creativity of language and the need for scientific evidence needs to be justified in language before a knowledgeable audience.

69 A further set of underlying tensions that might be identified are personal to the author of the passage.

70 It is easy to gain the impression that the author has had some bad experience, where the author's or a close friend's work was negatively critiqued on what they saw as spurious grounds.

Evolution

71 What did the parents of the factifuging passage look like?

72 Perhaps the father was a very formal, even pompous, student handout stating the need for very tightly reasoned, non-flowery and very sober language for 'proper' scientific reporting.

73 The mother may have been an ironic humour play akin to the TV programme *Blackadder*. The laws of survival for publication of this paper in the prestigious medical journal *The Lancet* require it to be written to a very high literacy standard, for the editor not to take him- or herself too seriously and to have the confidence to publish.

74 The passage appeared in a 'letter to the editor' section of the journal so its ironic take on scientific research methods was allowed to flourish in a different environment to the mainstream research articles.

Irony, paradox and humour

75 The passage would be ironic, in its most strict sense, if there was some chance that some readers thought it was serious.

76 There is some irony in that scientists do see a contradiction between the ideals of objective research and a game of one-upmanship between scientists.

77 There is a clash between the scientist as an impartial collector of facts and the scientist as a career bureaucrat. Aristotle recognised this in *Rhetoric* when he appreciated the need on occasion to flatter the audience during serious knowledge acquisition.

78 Many well-known scientists have been found to have 'fudged' their findings to better fit their careers or theories.

79 This all raises the more serious issue of whether we should assume scientists are unbiased or whether we should insist they make their bias explicit.

80 The passage is made humorous by revealing a contradiction between sincerity and saving face.

Reflection and consequences

81 From a consequences stance the passage reveals a tension between the conse-quences for the 'face' of the presenter of the apparently scientific evidence, and the consequences for science if the sceptical process enquiry is compromised.

82 The passage is reactive in that it states what to do in response to actions by the audience.

83 Responses are not recommended on the basis of the traditional steps of decision making, i.e. solicit all possible information on all possible solutions before making a reasoned decision that will benefit the greatest number of people.

Interrogative pronouns

Causes:

84 Why did it (the passage) happen? The perceived quality of research findings does seem to depend somewhat on the reputation of the finder.

85 What made it happen? Interesting or influential research findings do carry with them financial and status rewards.

86 Who made it happen? I am tempted to blame Ramas, an Elizabethan philoso-pher who seems to have initiated the idea that scientists should have the same ideals as priests, be pure of thought and in perfect servitude to their purpose in life. Both seem to be farcical.

87 With what instruments? The instrument used seems perfect for the job, statis-tics. It also carries the air of impartiality; can the number lie, let alone commit 'damn lies'?

Circumstances:

88 **When did it happen? The passage was written decades ago, and seems timeless.**

89 **Where did it happen? It happened in a synchronous peer review meeting. If the presenter was not so much on the spot in a public forum, then more considered responses may have been recommended.**

90 **How did it happen, in what circumstances? The more seasoned scientist is advising the novice presenter.**

Result:

91 **What happened? The passage author revealed the human side of scientific evidence and reputations.**

Emerging a new critique stance

The purpose of generating using multiple stances is to ensure the passage is better appreciated, more so than seeing it from only one stance. However, having all these multiple critique statements raises the question of how they might be used in some integrated way to provide a sort of meta critique. The reader is invited to think that one through for him- or herself but suggestions for emerging an integrated stance from the different statements follow. One rather unstructured approach would be to look through all the statements to see if some implicit theme or focus strikes you. Another slightly more structured approach has been suggested by Alexander (1964) who notes that ideas are networks, a synthesis of other ideas.

Alexander's method involves first numbering the statements, as was done above where there are ninety-one statements – more than enough. The statements should preferably be conditional truth statements, but it is not necessary to be too pedantic. Each statement represents an idea. Next, read a statement and distil some sort of essence from it, what it is about? For example, statement 28 says:

28   A politician would appreciate that good findings do not and should not speak for themselves; they have to be passionately argued for.

To me, the essence of this statement is something about persuasion and advocates. Then read through all the other statements looking for one that has roughly the same essence.

If you find one or more then these statements can be considered 'connected'. I think statement 5 is connected to statement 28. It too contains suggestions of persuasion and advocates.

> 5   Presentations of research findings will always include some insincere language games to persuade the audience not to expect the choice of language to be neutral.

This process of connecting statements should continue to a maximum of 10% of the possible connections. This means: only connect those statements that are strongly connected; avoid weak connections. This will again be a very personal choice and many statements may end up not connected. The connections can be drafted into a matrix (spreadsheet) which has the numbers of the statements (1 to 91) as both the left hand labels and along the top. For example:

	1	2	3	...	91
1			x		
2					
3	x				
⋮					
91					

This part of the 91 × 91 matrix shows the example of a connection recorded between statement 1 and statement 3. This matrix can then be shown graphically as a network diagram. The network diagram in Figure 13.1 shows the connections that I thought exist between many of the statements. It was drawn by providing the matrix to a piece of software called UNINET6 written by Analytic Technologies. The software has an advantage in being able to remember all the connections before it starts to situate the statement nodes into the diagram. It also allows for numerous calculations and adoptions to be performed on the network.

In the network diagram, the numbers are the statement numbers and the lines show what statements I thought were connected. For example, from 'top centre' you can see that statements 6 and 22, 6 and 74 and 6 and 89 were recorded as being connected. As predicted by the small world phenomenon (Watts, 1999), the network turns out to have 'clusters'; it is not evenly distributed. My interpretation is that there are three main clusters of statement numbers. One might be called 'top centre' and has statement numbers 28, 29, 45, 82, 89, 6, 74, 23. There is another which might be called 'bottom left' which includes 52, 55, 21, 4 and 5. The third might be called 'centre right' which includes statements 65, 43, 13, 34 and 26. You will remember that these three clusters are made up of critique statements from different stances. Statements 28 and 29 were

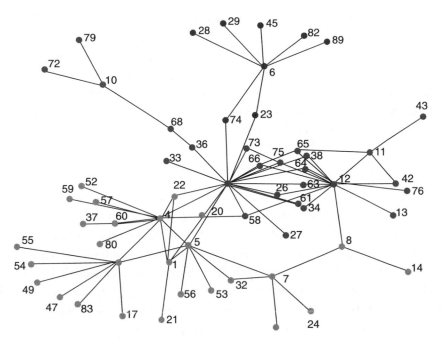

Figure 13.1   Network diagram

from the TO&P stance while 6 was from system thinking. Statement 74 was from the evolution stance. So, these three clusters can be thought of as the integration of parts of various stances.

The three clusters have the potential to provide 'emergent' stances. For example, consider the 'top centre' cluster made up of statements 74, 23, 28, 29, 45, 82, 89, 6. These statements can be randomly combined into a paragraph something like the following:

> a mathematician could see the passage as an example of the failure of everyday language for the creation of scientific knowledge (23) … The passage appeared in a 'letter to the editor' section of the journal so its ironic take on the scientific research methods was allowed to flourish in a different environment to the mainstream research articles (74) … a politician would appreciate that good findings do not and should not speak for themselves, they have to be passionately argued for (28) … the system may be the seminar circuit, or the scientific publication system or perhaps the academic careers system (45) … the classic example may be the laws of evolution which after 150 years of vigorous debate are still not fully accepted by the wider community (29) … the passage is reactive in that it states what to do in response to actions by the audience (82) … the system identified from the passage is the one that transforms private knowledge into public knowledge (6) … where did it happen? It happened in a synchronous peer review meeting. If the presenter was not so much on the spot in a public forum, then more considered responses may have been recommended (89) …

Reading this passage over a few times, not paying too much attention to particulars and letting my mind wander a bit, I start to think about 'humankind vs. science'. Science was intended to relieve us, humankind, from our suffering, to enlighten, to be our servant, to free us from superstition. But perhaps it has become the yoke we are all tied to, our hard taskmaster, the ends not the means. The science stance needs a lot more development but could be used to critique other passages. It will be used further in the next chapter on writing-up critiques.

Summary

This chapter began by demonstrating how different stances on the same passage generate different critique statements, following which, the passage is most likely better appreciated. Towards the end it demonstrated a method for combining statements from differing stances so as to try and emerge a new stance. This process might be said to use the left and right parts of the brain. Some aspects were prescriptive and analytical, while other aspects required leaps of personal synthesis interpretation. The system thinking literature suggests that this combination is creative.

14 Writing-Up Your Critique

Critique the following passage.

How to write a critique

1 Sit in a straight, comfortable chair in a well lit place with plenty of freshly sharpened pencils.
2 Read over the passage carefully, to make certain you understand it.
3 Walk down to the vending machines and buy some coffee to help you concentrate.
4 Stop off at another floor, on the way back, and visit your friend from class. If your friend hasn't started the paper yet either, you can both walk to McDonald's and buy a hamburger to help you concentrate. If your friend shows you his critique, typed, double-spaced, and bound in one of those irritating see-through plastic folders, drop him.
5 When you get back to your room, sit in a straight, comfortable chair in a clean, well lit place with plenty of freshly sharpened pencils.
6 Read over the passage again to make absolutely certain you understand it.
7 You know, you haven't written to that kid you met at camp since fourth grade. You'd better write that letter now and get it out of the way so you can concentrate.
8 Go look at your teeth in the bathroom mirror.
9 Listen to one side of your favourite tape and that's it. I mean it, as soon as it's over you are going to start that critique.
10 Listen to the other side.
11 Rearrange all of your CDs into alphabetical order.
12 Phone your friend on the other floor and ask if he's started writing yet. Exchange derogatory remarks about your teacher, the course, the university, the world at large.
13 Sit in a straight, comfortable chair in a clean, well lit place with plenty of freshly sharpened pencils.

(Continued)

(Continued)

14 Read over the passage again; roll the words across your tongue; savour its special flavour.

15 Check the newspaper listings to make sure you aren't missing something truly worthwhile on TV. NOTE: When you have a paper due in less than 12 hours, anything on TV from Masterpiece Theater to Sgt. Preston of the Yukon, is truly worthwhile, with these exceptions: Pro Bowler's Tour, any movie starring Don Ameche.

16 Catch the last hour of Soul Brother of Kung Fu on channel 26.

17 Phone your friend on the third floor to see if he was watching. Discuss the finer points of the plot.

18 Go look at your tongue in the bathroom mirror.

19 Look through your roommate's book of pictures from home. Ask who everyone is.

20 Sit down and do some serious thinking about your plans for the future.

21 Open your door and check to see if there are any mysterious, trench-coated strangers lurking in the hall.

22 Sit in a straight, comfortable chair in a clean, well lit place with plenty of freshly sharpened pencils.

23 Read over the passage one more time, just for the hell of it.

24 Scoot your chair across the room to the window and watch the sunrise.

25 Lie face down on the floor and moan.

26 Leap up and write the critique.

27 Type the critique.

28 Complain to everyone that you didn't get any sleep because you had to write the damn critique.

Source: unknown

All the previous chapters have, understandably, been about ways of reading. Having read a passage and noted some critique statements, you may want to, or be required to, provide a written critique. This takes us to a whole new problem: the structure of written critiques. Fortunately, written critiques can use the same stances as used for reading. Therefore, the advice below is something of a recursion of what has been presented in previous chapters, especially the argument chapter. For writing guides see web sites like Harvard's Writing Centre:

http://www.fas.harvard.edu/~wricntr/index.cgi?section=tools

Picking up on the final part of the previous chapter on multiple stances, the emerged stance was one about science being to assist and enlighten rather than being a burden or yoke. So let's assume that is being used to drive the written critique, to provide the argument.

The argument (conclusion, knowledge claim)

The argument is also the conclusion, conjecture, proposition or knowledge claim. State your argument at the beginning of the written critique so the reader can appreciate what and why the rest of the critique says what it does. Else you are asking the reader to read on not being sure why. Making the reader wait until the end is perhaps rude and optimistic. Many will not bother. A critique is not a mystery novel where 'who done it' is an inductive argument which gives amusement by emerging at the end. State your argument at the beginning and again at the end. Some writers also state the argument in the title. It can be reworded at the beginning as a question if preferred. For example, the argument: 'that science should enlighten much as art does' could be stated as 'Should not science enlighten as much as art does?'

Any argument (as a one-line conclusion) contains an object and at least two concerns (subjects). It is useful to identify these explicitly. In our example:

- *Object* = *science*

- *Concern 1: (perspective/subjective)* = enlightenment

- *Concern 2: art*

The second concern (art) is used to create dialectic; in this case the object under study, scientific research, against the arts (painting, literature and poetry). Making this clear will assist both the quality of your own writing and make it easier to read. As mentioned in the argument stance chapter, this is analogous to Galileo arguing against the idea that the sun goes around the earth. All arguments are against something but, if not made explicit, the justification of the argument can be unconvincing. If the argument was simply that science is good, and the justification excluded mention of inspiration, then artists would not be convinced.

It may next be worth reflecting on Popper's advice and asking yourself if your argument is novel and falsifiable. Novelty seems obvious enough; will your audience have heard your argument before, at least in the form and detail you intend to present? Falsification means is it likely anyone can or will argue against you. Having made it clear what you are arguing against will help here somewhat. In the science example it does seem possible that someone could bring evidence to show that science is oppressive; the study of mathematics and physical laws are but one example. That much of science has been to counter the impact of previous science is another possible example.

Having divided the argument into key words, it is useful to reflect on whether your intended audience will understand all these words in the same way you intend to use them. In the example, science, enlightenment and art may need some definition – and the exact definition of science may be central to justifying your argument.

The problem (motivation, importance)

Your critique will need to include some justification that the problem you are addressing is important. Reasoning, examples, or the comments of others may be used. This is something of a mark of respect for the reader, who has to decide whether your critique is worth his or her time to read. The debate between science and the arts could be argued as important because students have to choose careers in one rather than the other, and, as has been commented upon by many writers, because inspiration is as important as effort in enlightenment.

Supporting evidence

A critique should draw on the tools of science such as reasoning, experimentation, experience and explanations why. It should be ethical, honest and give voice to all those affected. You may want to think of it like a cross-examination in court. Not only can the evidence presented in the passage be critiqued but other evidence can be introduced. It will be unconvincing if you use your own opinions as the only supporting evidence unless you are reporting your own research findings. The chapter on how to use the argument stance to critique can also be used to help your thinking about what evidence will support your written critique.

Critiques differ from scientific or legal writing in that there is much more scope for artistic flare. This should not be confused with ignoring the rules of good supporting evidence, but there may be more room to appeal explicitly to more spiritual or inspirational aspects of people's lives. The collection of good-quality supporting evidence should not be confused with how it is presented. My advice is to write as if writing to yourself many years in the future (or the past), rather than as if you are writing something for your science teacher to grade.

The following critique has some flair. It is by Joseph Conrad, an ex-merchant seaman who will have seen a lot of sunsets, of the book *The Ascending Effort*, by George Bourne, relevant here because its argument is for the art of poetry not to be destroyed by science.

Much good paper has been lamentably wasted to prove that science has destroyed, that it is destroying, or, some day, may destroy poetry. Meantime, unblushing, unseen, and often unheard, the guileless poets have gone on singing in a sweet strain. How they dare do the impossible and virtually forbidden thing is a cause for wonder but not for legislation. Not yet. We are at present too busy reforming the silent burglar and planning concerts to soothe the savage breast of the yelling hooligan. As somebody, perhaps a publisher, said lately: Poetry is of no account now-a-days.

But it is not totally neglected. Those persons with gold-rimmed spectacles, whose usual occupation is to spy upon the obvious, have remarked audibly (on several occasions) that poetry has so far not given to science any acknowledgment worthy of its distinguished position in the popular mind. Except that Tennyson looked down the throat of a foxglove, that Erasmus Darwin wrote 'The Loves Of The Plants' and a scoffer 'The Loves Of The Triangles', poets have been supposed to be indecorously blind to the progress of science. What tribute, for instance, has poetry paid to electricity? All I can remember on the spur of the moment is Mr. Arthur Symons line about arc lamps: 'Hung with the globes of some unnatural fruit'.

Commerce and Manufacture praise on every hand in their not mute but inarticulate way the glories of science. Poetry does not play its part. Behold John Keats, skilful with the surgeon's knife; but when he writes poetry his inspiration is not from the operating table. Here I am reminded, though, of a modern instance to the contrary in prose. Mr. H. G. Wells, who, as far as I know, has never written a line of verse, was inspired a few years ago to write a short story, 'Under The Knife.' Out of a clock-dial, a brass rod, and a whiff of chloroform, he has conjured for us a sensation of space and eternity, evoked the face of the Unknowable, and an awesome, august voice, like the voice of the Judgment Day; a great voice, perhaps the voice of science itself, uttering the words: There shall be no more pain! I advise you to look up that story, so human and so intimate, because Mr. Wells, the writer of prose whose amazing inventiveness we all know, remains a poet even in his most perverse moments of scorn for things as they are. His poetic imagination is sometimes even greater than his inventiveness, I am not afraid to say. But, indeed, imaginative faculty would make any man a poet were he born without tongue for speech and without hands to seize his fancy and fasten her down to a wretched piece of paper.

The book (*The Ascending Effort*, by George Bourne) which in the course of the last few days I have opened and shut several times is not imaginative. But, on the other hand, it is not a dumb book, as some are. It has even a sort of sober and serious eloquence, reminding us that not poetry alone is at fault in this matter. Mr. Bourne begins his 'Ascending Effort' with a remark by Sir Francis Galton upon Eugenics that if the principles he was advocating were to become effective they

(Continued)

(Continued)

must be introduced into the national conscience, like a new religion. Introduced suggests compulsory vaccination. Mr. Bourne, who is not a theologian, wishes to league together not science and religion, but science and the arts. The intoxicating power of art, he thinks, is the very thing needed to give the desired effect to the doctrines of science. In uninspired phrase he points to the arts playing once upon a time a part in popularising the Christian tenets. With painstaking fervour as great as the fervour of prophets, but not so persuasive, he foresees the arts some day popularising science. Until that day dawns, science will continue to be lame and poetry blind. He himself cannot smooth or even point out the way, though he thinks that a really prudent people would be greedy of beauty, and their public authorities as careful of the sense of comfort as of sanitation.

As the writer of those remarkable rustic notebooks, 'The Bettesworth Book' and 'Memoirs Of A Surrey Labourer', the author has a claim upon our attention. But his seriousness, his patience, his almost touching sincerity, can only command the respect of his readers and nothing more. He is obsessed by science, haunted and shadowed by it, until he has been bewildered into awe. He knows, indeed, that art owes its triumphs and its subtle influence to the fact that it issues straight from our organic vitality, and is a movement of life-cells with their matchless unintellectual knowledge. But the fact that poetry does not seem obviously in love with science has never made him doubt whether it may not be an argument against his haste to see the marriage ceremony performed amid public rejoicings.

Many a man has heard or read and believes that the earth goes round the sun; one small blob of mud among several others, spinning ridiculously with a waggling motion like a top about to fall. This is the Copernican system, and the man believes in the system without often knowing as much about it as its name. But while watching a sunset he sheds his belief; he sees the sun as a small and useful object, the servant of his needs and the witness of his ascending effort, sinking slowly behind a range of mountains, and then he holds the system of Ptolemy. He holds it without knowing it. In the same way a poet hears, reads, and believes a thousand undeniable truths which have not yet got into his blood, nor will do after reading Mr. Bourne's book; he writes, therefore, as if neither truths nor book existed. Life and the arts follow dark courses, and will not turn aside to the brilliant arc-lights of science. Some day, without a doubt, and it may be a consolation to Mr. Bourne to know it, fully informed critics will point out that Mr. Davies' poem on a dark woman combing her hair must have been written after the invasion of appendicitis, and that Mr. Yeats 'Had I the heaven's embroidered cloths' came before radium was quite unnecessarily dragged out of its respectable obscurity in pitchblende to upset the venerable (and comparatively naive) chemistry of our young days.

There are times when the tyranny of science and the cant of science are alarming, but there are other times when they are entertaining – and this is one of them.

Many a man prides himself, says Mr. Bourne, on his piety or his views of art, whose whole range of ideas, could they be investigated, would be found ordinary, if not base, because they have been adopted in compliance with some external persuasion or to serve some timid purpose instead of proceeding authoritatively from the living selection of his hereditary taste. This extract is a fair sample of the book's thought and of its style. But Mr. Bourne seems to forget that persuasion is a vain thing. The appreciation of great art comes from within.

It is but the merest justice to say that the transparent honesty of Mr. Bourne's purpose is undeniable. But the whole book is simply an earnest expression of a pious wish; and, like the generality of pious wishes, this one seems of little dynamic value besides being impracticable.

Yes, indeed. Art has served Religion; artists have found the most exalted inspiration in Christianity; but the light of Transfiguration which has illuminated the profoundest mysteries of our sinful souls is not the light of the generating stations, which exposes the depths of our infatuation where our mere cleverness is permitted for a while to grope for the unessential among invincible shadows.

Source: Joseph Conrad (2003) 'The Ascending Effort',
1910, in *Notes on Life and Letters*

Notes

1 The word 'argument' is used in two ways, as the conclusion and also as supporting evidence. The other sees the argument as a one-liner, similar to the conclusion. The one-liner convention is used in this book.
2 Experience received through the senses.
3 To be contrasted with 'in theory', which means 'hopefully' or 'ideally'.
4 The alternative view at the time was that international trade was the key to innovation and the reduction of poverty.
5 All this interest in caterpillars and nature was partly because of a high level of interest in biology at the time stimulated by Darwin's recent publication of his theory of evolution.
6 http://skeptic.com/positivism.html.
7 This chapter makes extensive use of Tony Hookins' research (Hookins, 2005).
8 Aristotle, *Nicomachean Ethics*, book 3, section 1.
9 Walther, H. *Proverbia sententiaeque Latinitatis Medii Aevi: Lateinische Sprichwörter und Sentenzen des Mittelalters in alphabetischer Anordnung*. 6 vols. Göttingen: Vandenhoeck & Ruprecht, 1963. Entry 25432, variants at 25428–25432.
10 From the Latin: *factum*, act, deed, or 'fact'; *fugare*, to put to flight (cf. febrifuge, vermifuge).

References

Ackoff, R. (2000). Making a Difference, Systems Thinking/Systems Change: http://a2j. kent law.edu/Presentations/GirlsLink/index.html.

Aerts, D., L. Apostel, et al. (1994). *Worldviews: From Fragmentation to Integration*. Brussels, VUB Press.

Alexander, C. (1964). *Notes on the Synthesis of Form*. Cambridge, MA, Harvard University Press.

Allport, G. (1954). *The nature of prejudice*. Reading, MA, Addison-Wesley.

Argyris, C. and D. A. Schon (1978). *Theory in Practice*. San Francisco, Jossey-Bass.

Argyris, C. and D. A. Schon (1996). *Organisational Learning II*. Reading MA, Addison-Wesley.

Armstrong, J., Ed. (2000). *Principles of Forecasting*. Norwell, MA, Kluwer.

Arnold, M. (2003). On the Phenomenology of Technology. *Information and Organization* 13: 231–256.

Baker, R. (2000). *Sperm Wars*. London, Pan.

Barnes, B. and D. Bloor (1982). Relativism, Rationalism and the Sociology of Knowledge. *Rationality and Rationalism*. Ed. M. Hollis and S. Lukes. Oxford, Basil Blackwell: 21–47.

Boulding, K. E. (1956). General Systems Theory – The Skeleton of Science. *Management Science* 2(3): 197–208.

Bowles, F. E. and M. J. A. Parkinson (1995). Measuring Audit Performance: Are the Instruments Fine Enough? *Computer Audit Journal* 3: 20–28.

Bronte-Stewart, M. (1999). Regarding Rich Pictures as Tools for Communication in Information Systems Development. *Computing and Information Systems* 6: 83–102.

Camazine, S., J.-L. Deneubourg, et al. (2001). *Self-Organization in Biological Systems*. Princeton, NJ, Princeton University Press.

Carroll, L. (1939). *The Complete Works of Lewis Carroll*. London, The Nonesuch Press.

Carson, L. J. (2003). Understanding Dialogue: To a Unified Field Part I. *Anchor Point* 17(11): http://www.nlpanchorpoint.com/Carson-DialogII1453.pdf.

Chalmers, A. F. (1982). *What Is this Thing Called Science*. Brisbane, University of Queensland Press.

Checkland, P. (2000). Soft Systems Methodology: A Thirty Year Retrospective. *Systems Research and Behavioural Science* 17(1): S11–S58.

Churchman, C. W. (1971). *The Design of Inquiring Systems*. New York, John Wiley & Sons.

Cohen, H. F. (1994). *The Scientific Revolution: A Historiographical Inquiry*. Chicago, University of Chicago Press.

Conrad, J. (2003). *Notes on Life and Letters*. Edited by J. H. Stape. Cambridge, Cambridge University Press.

Crosswhite, J. (1996). *The Rhetoric of Reason*. Madison, University of Wisconsin Press.

Daellenbach, H. and R. L. Flood (2002). *The Informed Student Guide to Management Science*. London, Thomson Learning.

Dawkins, R. (1989). *The Selfish Gene*. Oxford, Oxford University Press.

Dawson, R. (2000). *Power Negotiating for Salespeople: Inside Secrets From a Master Negotiator*, New Jersey Career Press.

Dennett, D. C. (1989). *The Intentional Stance*. Cambridge, MA, MIT Press.

Dennett, D. C. (1996). *Darwin's Dangerous Idea*. New York, Touchstone.

Dewey, J. (1910). *How We Think*. New York, Dover.

Eemeren, F. H. and R. Grootendorst (2003). Pragma-dialectical Procedure for a Critical Discussion. *Argumentation* 17: 365–386.

Eemeren, F. H., R. Grootendorst, et al. (1987). *Handbook of Argumentation Theory*. Dordrecht, Foris Publications.

Foucault, M. (1973). *This is Not a Pipe*. Translated by James Harkness. Berkeley, University of California Press.

Galilei, G. (2001). *Dialogues Concerning Two New Sciences*. New York, William Andrew Publishing.

Gao, J. (2005). Problem Picturing. PhD Thesis. University of South Australia.

Gilbert, D. T. (1991). How Mental Systems Believe. *American Psychologist* 46(2): 107–119.

Gorman, J. (1988). *The Man With No Endorphins*. New York, Viking Adult.

Guindon, R. (1990). Designing the Design Process. *Human Computer Interaction* 5: 305–344.

Habermas, J. (1968). *Knowledge and Human Interests*. Boston, MA, Beacon.

Hanson, N. R. (1971). *Observation and Explanation*. New York, Harper & Row.

Hatch, M. J. (1997). Irony and the Social Construction of Contradiction. *Organization Science* 8(3): 275–288.

Hatch, M. J. and S. B. Ehrlich (1993). Spontaneous Humour and an Indicator of Paradox and Ambiguity in Organizations. *Organization Studies* 14(4): 505–526.

Haynes, J. (2000). *Perspectival Thinking*. New Zealand, ThisOne and Company.

Hofstadter, D. (1979). *Godel, Escher, Bach: An Eternal Golden Braid*. London, Penguin.

Hookins, T. (2005). Developing a Questioning Model. PhD Thesis. University of South Australia.

James, W. (1907/1910). *Pragmatism*. Cleveland, World Publishing (Meridian).

Jensen, J. V. (1978). A Heuristic for the Analysis of the Nature and Extent of a Problem. *Journal of Creative Behaviour* 12(3): 169–181.

Kahneman, D., A. Tversky, et al. (1982). *Judgment Under Uncertainty*. Cambridge, Cambridge University Press.

Keen, P. (2000). Staff Seminar. Georgia State University, Atlanta.

Kelly, W. E. (2002). An Investigation of Worry and Sense of Humor. *Journal of Psychology* 136(6): 657–666.

Kepner, C. and Tregoe, B. (1997). *The New Rational Manager: An Updated Edition for a New World*. Princeton, NJ, Princeton University Press.

Kipling, R. (1988[1902]). The Elephant's Child in *Just So Stories*. London, Voyager Books.

Klein, G. A. (1989). *Recognition Primed Decisions. Advances in Man-Machine Systems Research*. Ed. W. B. Rouse. Greenwich, CT, JAI Press, 5: 47–92.

Lahoff, G. (1993). The Contemporary Theory of Metaphor. In *Metaphor and Thought*. Ed. A. Ortney. Cambridge, Cambridge University Press: 202–251.

Landry, M. (1995). A Note on the Concept of Problem. *Organizational Studies* 16(2): 315–327.

Latour, B. (1986). Visualization and Cognition. *Knowledge and Society* 6: 1–40.

Lewis, M. W. (2000). Exploring Paradox: Towards a More Comprehensive Guide. *Academy of Management Review* 25(4): 760–776.

Liebl, F. (2002). The Anatomy of Complex Societal Problems. *Journal of the Operational Research Society* 53: 161–184.

Linstone, H. A. (1999). *Decision Making for Technology Executives: Using Multiple Perspectives*. Boston, Artech House.

Lisnek, P. and Oliver, E. (2001). *Courtroom Power: Communication Strategies for Trial Lawyers*, Eau Claire, WI, Pesi Law Publications.

List, D. and M. Metcalfe (2004). Sourcing Forecast Knowledge Through Argumentative Inquiry. *Technological Forecasting and Social Change* 71: 525–535.

Maio Makay, M. and M. Metcalfe (2001). Multiple Method Forecasts for Discontinuous Innovations, *Technological Forecasting and Social Change* 69: 221–232.

Mason, D. (1994). Planning an English Course for Students of Health Care; http://exchanges. state.gov/forum/vols/vol32/no2/#special_ret_41, 32(2): 18.

Mason, R. O. (1969). A Dialectical Approach to Strategic Planning. *Management Science* 15: B-403–B-414.

Mason, R. O. (1996). Commentary of Varieties of Dialectic Change Processes. *Journal of Management Inquiry* 5(3): 293–300.

McGhee, P. E. (1979). *Humor: Its Origins and Development*. New York, Freeman.

Metcalfe, M. and P. Powell (1995). Perceiver's Concerns: On the Nature of Information. International Symposium on 5th Generation Computer Systems, Tokyo.

Midgley, G., Ed. (2003). *Systems Thinking*, Sage Library in Business and Management. London, Sage.

Milgram, S., Ed. (1992). *The Individual in a Social World: Essays and Experiments*. New York, McGraw-Hill.

Miller, G. A. (1956). The Magical Number Seven, Plus or Minus Two: Some Limits on Our Capacity for Processing Information. *The Psychological Review* 63: 81–97.

Mintzberg, H. and F. Westley (2001). It's Not What You Think. *Sloan Management Review* Spring: 89–93.

Mitroff, I. and H. Linstone (1993). *The Unbounded Mind: Breaking the Chains of Traditional Business Thinking*. Oxford, Oxford University Press.

Morgan, G. (1986). *Images of Organisations*. Thousand Oaks, CA, Sage.

Muecke, D. C. (1982). *Irony and the Ironic*. London, Methuen.

Newell, A. and H. A. Simon (1972). *Human Problem Solving*. New York, Prentice Hall.

Nielsen, R. P. (1996). Varieties of Dialectic Change Processes. *Journal of Management Inquiry* 5(3): 276–293.

Ortney, A. (1975). Why metaphors are necessary and not just nice. *Educational Theory* 25: 45–53.

Oswick, C., T. Keenoy et al. (2002). Metaphor and Analogical Reasoning in Organization Theory. *Academy of Management Review* 27(2): 294–303.

Overduff, J. and Silverhorn, J. (1996). Beyond Words: Languaging Change Through the Quantum Field. Audio Tapes. Neuro-Energetics, Washington Boro, PA.

Pepper, S. C. (1942). *World Hypotheses: A study in evidence*. Berkeley, CA, University of California Press.

Perelman, C. and L. Olbrechts-Tyteca (1969). The New Rhetoric: A Treatise on Argumentation. Paris, University of Notre Dame.

Polanyi, M. (1966). *The Tacit Dimension*. Garden City, NY, Doubleday.

Polya, G. (1945). *How To Solve It*. Princeton, NJ, Princeton University Press.

Poole, M. S. and A. Van de Ven (1989). Using Paradox to Build Management and Organizational Theories. *Academy of Management Review* 14(4): 562–578.

Popper, K. R. (1963). *Conjectures and Refutations: The Growth of Scientific Knowledge*. London, Routledge & Kegan Paul.

Purcell, F. J. B. (2000). *Value Engineering: A Tool for Our Times*. Boynton Beach, FL. Purcell Associates.

Quine, W. V. (1961). *The Ways of Paradox*. New York, Random House.

Richards, L. A. (1936). *The Philosophy of Rhetoric*. New York, Oxford University Press.

Rorty, R. (1989). *Contingency, Irony and Solidarity*. Cambridge, Cambridge University Press.

Sowell, T. (1985). *Marxism*. London, Unwin.

Snow, C. P. (1993). *The Two Cultures*. Cambridge, Cambridge University Press.

Toulmin, S. (1964). *The Uses of Argument*, Cambridge, Cambridge University Press.

Ulrich, W. (1983). *Critical Heuristics of Social Planning: A New Approach to Practical Philosophy*. Chichester, John Wiley & Sons.

Walton, D. (1998). *The New Dialectic*, Toronto, Toronto University Press.

Watts, D. J. (1999). Networks, Dynamics and the Small World Phenomenon. *American Journal of Sociology* 105(2): 493–527.

Watzlawick, P., J. B. Bavelas and D. D. Jackson (1967). *Pragmatics of Human Communication: A Study of Interactional Patterns, Pathologies and Paradoxes*. New York, W.W. Norton.

Werhane, P. H. (2002). Moral Imagination and Systems Thinking. *Journal of Business Ethics* 38: 33–42.

Whetten, D. A. (1989). What Constitutes a Theoretical Contribution. *Academy of Management Review* 14(4): 490–495.

Wicklund, R. A. (1999). Multiple Perspectives in Person Perception and Theorizing. *Theory and Psychology* 9(5): 667–678.

Wilson, P. (1983). *Second Hand Knowledge*. Westport, CT, Greenwood Press.

Yardley, G. and J. Kelly (1995). *NLP Practitioners Handbook*. Singapore, Southern Lands NLP.

Index

Added to a page number, 'f' denotes a figure.